Pastoral Letters *and* The Letter *to the* Hebrews

1 AND 2 TIMOTHY, TITUS, HEBREWS

WILLIAM A. ANDERSON, DMIN, PHD

Liguori
LIGUORI, MISSOURI

Imprimi Potest:
Harry Grile, CSsR, Provincial
Denver Province, The Redemptorists

Printed with Ecclesiastical Permission and Approved for Private or Instructional Use
Nihil Obstat: Rev. Msgr. Kevin Michael Quirk, JCD, JV
      Censor Librorum
      Imprimatur: +Michael J. Bransfield
      Bishop of Wheeling-Charleston [West Virginia]
July 15, 2013

Published by Liguori Publications
Liguori, Missouri 63057

To order, call 800-325-9521
www.liguori.org

Cataloging-in-Publication Data on file with the Library of Congress

p ISBN 978-0-7648-2128-8
e ISBN 978-0-7648-6925-9

Liguori Publications, a nonprofit corporation, is an apostolate of The Redemptorists. To learn more about The Redemptorists, visit Redemptorists.com.

Printed in the United States of America
18 17 16 15 14 / 5 4 3 2 1
First Edition

Contents

NOTE: The length of each Bible section varies. Group leaders should combine sections as needed to fit the number of sessions in their program.

Dedication

THIS SERIES is lovingly dedicated to the memory of my parents, Kathleen and Angor Anderson, in gratitude for all they shared with all who knew them, especially my siblings and me.

Acknowledgments

BIBLE STUDIES and reflections depend on the help of others who read the manuscript and make suggestions. I am especially indebted to Sister Anne Francis Bartus, CSJ, DMin, whose vast experience and knowledge were very helpful in bringing this series to its final form.

Introduction to
Liguori Catholic Bible Study

READING THE BIBLE can be daunting. It's a complex book, and many a person of goodwill has tried to read the Bible and ended up putting it down in utter confusion. It helps to have a companion, and *Liguori Catholic Bible Study* is a solid one. Over the course of this series, you'll learn about biblical messages, themes, personalities, and events and understand how the books of the Bible rose out of the need to address new situations.

Across the centuries, people of faith have asked, "Where is God in this moment?" Millions of Catholics look to the Bible for encouragement in their journey of faith. Wisdom teaches us not to undertake Bible study alone, disconnected from the Church that was given Scripture to share and treasure. When used as a source of prayer and thoughtful reflection, the Bible comes alive.

Your choice of a Bible-study program should be dictated by what you want to get out of it. One goal of *Liguori Catholic Bible Study* is to give readers greater familiarity with the Bible's structure, themes, personalities, and message. But that's not enough. This program will also teach you to use Scripture in your prayer. God's message is as compelling and urgent today as ever, but we get only part of the message when it's memorized and stuck in our head. It's meant for the entire person—physical, emotional, and spiritual.

We're baptized into life with Christ, and we're called to live more fully with Christ today as we practice the values of justice, peace, forgiveness, and community. God's new covenant was written on the hearts of the people of Israel; we, their spiritual descendants, are loved that intimately by God today. *Liguori Catholic Bible Study* will draw you closer to God, in whose image and likeness we are fashioned.

Group and Individual Study

The *Liguori Catholic Bible Study* series is intended for group and individual study and prayer. This series gives you the tools to start a study group. Gathering two or three people in a home or announcing the meeting of a Bible-study group in a parish or community can bring surprising results. Each lesson in this series contains a section to help groups study, reflect, pray, and share biblical reflections. Each lesson, except the first, also has a second section for individual study.

Many people who want to learn more about the Bible don't know where to begin. This series gives them a place to start and helps them continue until they're familiar with all the books of the Bible.

Bible study can be a lifelong project, always enriching those who wish to be faithful to God's Word. When people complete a study of the whole Bible, they can begin again, making new discoveries with each new adventure into the Word of God.

Lectio Divina
(Sacred Reading)

BIBLE STUDY isn't just a matter of gaining intellectual knowledge of the Bible; it's also about gaining a greater understanding of God's love and concern for creation. The purpose of reading and knowing the Bible is to enrich our relationship with God. God loves us and gave us the Bible to illustrate that love. In his April 12, 2013, address before the Pontifical Biblical Commission, Pope Francis stressed that "the Church's life and mission are founded on the word of God which is the soul of theology and at the same time inspires the whole of Christian life."

The Meaning of *Lectio Divina*

Lectio divina is a Latin expression that means "divine or sacred reading." The process for *lectio divina* consists of Scripture readings, reflection, and prayer. Many clergy, religious, and laity use *lectio divina* in their daily spiritual reading to develop a closer and more loving relationship with God. Learning about Scripture has as its purpose the living of its message, which demands a period of reflection on the Scripture passages.

Prayer and *Lectio Divina*

Prayer is a necessary element for the practice of *lectio divina*. The entire process of reading and reflecting is a prayer. It's not merely an intellectual pursuit; it's also a spiritual one. Page 18 includes an Opening Prayer for gathering one's thoughts before moving on to the passages in each section. This prayer may be used privately or in a group. For those who use the book for daily spiritual reading, the prayer for each section may be repeated each day. Some may wish to keep a journal of each day's meditation.

Pondering the Word of God

Lectio divina is the ancient Christian spiritual practice of reading the holy Scriptures with intentionality and devotion. This practice helps Christians center themselves and descend to the level of the heart to enter an inner quiet space, finding God.

This sacred reading is distinct from reading for knowledge or information, and it's more than the pious practice of spiritual reading. It is the practice of opening ourselves to the action and inspiration of the Holy Spirit. As we intentionally focus on and become present to the inner meaning of the Scripture passage, the Holy Spirit enlightens our minds and hearts. We come to the text willing to be influenced by a deeper meaning that lies within the words and thoughts we ponder.

In this space, we open ourselves to be challenged and changed by the inner meaning we experience. We approach the text in a spirit of faith and obedience as a disciple ready to be taught by the Holy Spirit. As we savor the sacred text, we let go of our usual control of how we expect God to act in our lives and surrender our hearts and consciences to the flow of the divine (*divina*) through the reading (*lectio*).

The fundamental principle of *lectio divina* leads us to understand the profound mystery of the Incarnation, "The Word became flesh," not only in history but also within us.

Praying *Lectio* Today

Before you begin, relax your body and maintain a posture of prayer (back straight, eyes shut, feet flat on the floor). Then practice these four simple actions:

1. Read a passage from Scripture or the daily Mass readings. This is known as *lectio*. (If the Word of God is read aloud, the hearers listen attentively.)

2. Pray the selected passage with attention as you listen for a specific meaning that comes to mind. Once again, the reading is listened to or silently read and reflected or meditated on. This is known as *meditatio*.

3. The exercise becomes active. Pick a word, sentence, or idea that surfaces from your consideration of the chosen text. Does the reading remind you of a person, place, or experience? If so, pray about it. Compose your thoughts and reflection into a simple word or phrase. This prayer-thought will help you remove distractions during the *lectio*. This exercise is called *oratio*.

4. In silence, with your eyes closed, quiet yourself and become conscious of your breathing. Let your thoughts, feelings, and concerns fade as you consider the selected passage in the previous step (*oratio*). If you're distracted, use your prayer word to help you return to silence. This is *contemplatio*.

This exercise can take as long as you want, but in the context of this Bible study, 10 to 20 minutes should be sufficient.

Many teachers of prayer call contemplation the prayer of resting in God, a prelude to losing oneself in the presence of God. Scripture is transformed in our hearing as we pray and allow our hearts to unite intimately with the Lord. The Word truly takes on flesh, and this time it is manifested in our flesh.

How to Use This Bible-Study Companion

THE BIBLE, along with the commentaries and reflections found in this study, will help participants become familiar with the Scripture texts and lead them to reflect more deeply on the texts' message. At the end of this study, participants will have a firm grasp of the Pastoral Letters and the Letter to the Hebrews, becoming more cognizant of the spiritual nourishment these letters offer. This study is not only an intellectual adventure, it's also a spiritual one. The reflections lead participants into their own journey with the Scripture readings.

Context

When the authors wrote and edited the Pastoral Letters and the Letter to the Hebrews, they were dealing with later developments within Christianity that earlier writers of the New Testament did not address. To help readers learn about each passage in relation to those around it, each lesson begins with an overview that puts the Scripture passages into context.

Part 1: Group Study

To give participants a comprehensive study of the Pastoral Letters and the Letter to the Hebrews, the book is divided into six lessons. Lesson 1 is group study only; Lessons 2 through 6 are divided into two parts: group study and individual study. For example, Lesson 2 covers 1 Timothy 3—6. The study group reads and discusses only Chapters 3 and 4 (Part 1). Participants privately read and reflect on Chapters 5 and 6 (Part 2).

Group study may or may not include *lectio divina*. With *lectio divina*, the group meets for ninety minutes using the first format on page 16. Without *lectio divina*, the group meets for one hour using the second format on page 16, and participants are urged to privately read the *lectio divina* section at the end of Part 1. It contains additional reflections on the Scripture passages studied during the group session that will take participants even further into the passages.

Part 2: Individual Study

The passages not covered in Part 1 are divided into shorter components, one to be studied each day. Participants who don't belong to a study group can use the lessons for private sacred reading. They may choose to reflect on one Scripture passage per day, making it possible for a clearer understanding of the Scripture passages used in their *lectio divina* (sacred reading).

A PROCESS FOR SACRED READING

Liguori Publications has designed this study to be user friendly and manageable. However, group dynamics and leaders vary. We're not trying to keep the Holy Spirit from working in your midst, thus we suggest you decide beforehand which format works best for your group. If you have limited time, you could study the Bible as a group and save prayer and reflection for personal time.

However, if your group wishes to digest and feast on sacred Scripture through both prayer and study, we recommend you spend closer to ninety minutes each week by gathering to study and pray with Scripture. *Lectio divina* (see page 11) is an ancient contemplative prayer form that moves readers from the head to the heart in meeting the Lord. We strongly suggest using this prayer form whether in individual or group study.

GROUP-STUDY FORMATS

1. Bible Study With *Lectio Divina*

About ninety minutes of group study

- ✠ Gathering and opening prayer (3–5 minutes)
- ✠ Scripture passage read aloud (5 minutes)
- ✠ Silently review the commentary and prepare to discuss it with the group (3–5 minutes)
- ✠ Discuss the Scripture passage along with the commentary and reflection (30 minutes)
- ✠ Scripture passage read aloud a second time, followed by quiet time for meditation and contemplation (5 minutes)
- ✠ Spend some time in prayer with the selected passage. Group participants will slowly read the Scripture passage a third time in silence, listening for the voice of God as they read (10–20 minutes)
- ✠ Shared reflection (10–15 minutes)
- ✠ Closing prayer (3–5 minutes)

To become acquainted with lectio divina, *see page 11.*

2. Bible Study

About one hour of group study

- ✠ Gathering and opening prayer (3–5 minutes)
- ✠ Scripture passage read aloud (5 minutes)
- ✠ Silently review the commentary and prepare to discuss it with the group (3–5 minutes)
- ✠ Discuss the Scripture passage along with the commentary and reflection (40 minutes)
- ✠ Closing prayer (3–5 minutes)

Notes to the Leader

- ✠ Bring a copy of the *New American Bible,* revised edition.
- ✠ Plan which sections will be covered each week of your Bible study.
- ✠ Read the material in advance of each session.
- ✠ Establish written ground rules. (Example: We won't keep you longer than ninety minutes; don't dominate the sharing by arguing or debating.)
- ✠ Meet in an appropriate and welcoming gathering space (church building, meeting room, house).
- ✠ Provide name tags and perhaps use a brief icebreaker for the first meeting; ask participants to introduce themselves.
- ✠ Mark the Scripture passage(s) that will be read during the session.
- ✠ Decide how you would like the Scripture to be read aloud (whether by one or multiple readers).
- ✠ Use a clock or watch.
- ✠ Provide extra Bibles (or copies of the Scripture passages) for participants who don't bring their Bible.
- ✠ Ask participants to read the introduction (page 19) before the first session.
- ✠ Tell participants which passages to study and urge them to read the passages and commentaries before the meeting.
- ✠ If you opt to use the *lectio divina* format, familiarize yourself with this prayer form ahead of time.

Notes to Participants

- ✠ Bring a copy of the *New American Bible,* revised edition.
- ✠ Read the introduction (page 19) before the first session.
- ✠ Read the Scripture passages and commentaries before each session.
- ✠ Be prepared to share and listen respectfully. (This is not a time to debate beliefs or argue.)

Opening Prayer

Leader: O God, come to my assistance.

Response: O Lord, make haste to help me.

Leader: Glory be to the Father, and to the Son, and to the Holy Spirit...

Response: ...as it was in the beginning, is now, and ever shall be, world without end. Amen.

Leader: Christ is the vine and we are the branches. As branches linked to Jesus, the vine, we are called to recognize that the Scriptures are always being fulfilled in our lives. It is the living Word of God living on in us. Come, Holy Spirit, fill the hearts of your faithful and kindle in us the fire of your divine wisdom, knowledge, and love.

Response: Open our minds and hearts as we study your great love for us as shown in the Bible.

Reader: (Open your Bible to the assigned Scripture(s) and read in a paced, deliberate manner. Pause for one minute, listening for a word, phrase, or image that you may use in your *lectio divina* practice.)

Closing Prayer

Leader: Let us pray as Jesus taught us.

Response: Our Father...

Leader: Lord, inspire us with your Spirit as we study your Word in the Bible. Be with us this day and every day as we strive to know you and serve you and to love as you love. We believe that through your goodness and love, the Spirit of the Lord is truly upon us. Allow the words of the Bible, your Word, to capture us and inspire us to live as you live and to love as you love.

Response: Amen.

Leader: May the divine assistance remain with us always.

Response: In the name of the Father, and of the Son, and of the Holy Spirit. Amen.

Pastoral Letters and The Letter to the Hebrews

BESIDES THE PASTORAL LETTERS, this volume of the *Liguori Catholic Bible Study* series also contains the book of Hebrews, which is not one of the Pastoral Letters but which contains a theological message about Jesus and the gifts we receive through him. Like the Pastorals, it was a later letter, written around the end of the first century.

Read the overview for each letter before studying the letter.

PASTORAL LETTERS: 1 AND 2 TIMOTHY, TITUS

A woman was sitting on a park bench alongside a bicycle path when a boy of about fifteen years of age came riding toward her on his bike. When she saw him, she thought of her own son who was about the age of the boy and who was off with his friends, bicycling in a different part of town. She knew her son was growing up and needed to be with his friends, but she was a mother and did not like the idea of his becoming an adult. In her mind, he was growing up too fast, but she also knew that she had to allow him to move along in life. She laughed at her feelings and said to herself, "After all, I am a mother."

Just then, the boy on the bike was on the path in front of her. A small knapsack tied precariously to the back of the bike seat was falling to the side and, just as the boy was passing her, it fell off. The boy retrieved his knapsack and made several attempts to reattach it to the bike. Each time he thought he had it tied securely, it would sag to one side or the other.

The woman went over to the boy and said, "Let me show you how to do it." She had done it enough for her own son. She tied the knapsack to the back of the bike by centering it behind the seat.

When she had finished, the boy asked, "Why did you do that for me?"

The woman, surprised at the question, answered, "I don't know. You had trouble; I knew how to fix it. That's all! Besides, I had something to share with you, and I wanted to share it!" As the boy rode away, the woman continued to think about his question, and she said to herself, "After all, I am a mother."

Three letters in the New Testament (1 Timothy, 2 Timothy, and Titus) are known as the Pastoral Letters. They are basically letters from pastors to other pastors. Although we do not know the occasion for the letters, we can recognize from internal evidence that the authors were showing concern for the developments occurring within the Church. Like the mother in the opening story, they realized that the Church was growing and they wanted to assure themselves that as the Church matured, the message of Christ would always be central to its development.

In the letters, we meet an author who claims to be Paul the Apostle and who has great love for a Church that was developing with the times.

The name *Pastoral Letters*

The name *Pastoral* comes from the Latin word *pastor*, which can mean "shepherd," i.e., one who is a spiritual leader. Jesus was the "Good Shepherd," the perfect pastor. The Pastoral Letters stress the emerging roles of spiritual leadership in Church matters and address the establishment of a structure needed to deal with the growing numbers of people joining the Church. When these letters were written, the Church had moved from a concept of a united group of local assemblies to a more universal concept of Church.

Because the first generation of Christians—among them the original twelve apostles—was dying, an urgent need to develop an apostolic tradition was becoming more evident. Leaders had to pass their leadership on to others in order for the Church to survive. The pastorals provide directives for maintaining a common lifestyle within the early Christian community, a lifestyle based on the original teaching of the apostles and the early disciples, yet one that recognized a need for establishing norms for leadership within the Church.

Author

From the late second century until the nineteenth, scripture scholars considered Paul to be the author of these pastorals, since the author identifies himself as Paul in the first lines of the pastorals. In the early nineteenth century, however, most scholars came to believe that Paul did not write the letters, and that the author was an unknown Christian familiar with Paul's writings. When the author or authors of the pastorals wrote their letters, Paul's writings had become well known among many Christian communities. The First Letter to Timothy and the Letter to Titus are more formal in content than the Second Letter to Timothy, a fact which may point to a different author for Second Timothy, although the letter treats similar themes.

The custom of identifying oneself by another's name was an accepted custom during the time in which the Scriptures were written. The use of Paul's name indicates that the author believed that he was faithful to the teachings of the apostle, who was most likely dead at the time the pastorals were written. If the letter sounded like it came from the pen of Paul, very few would object to the author's using Paul's name.

Since the author sounds so much like Paul, it becomes difficult to comment on the letter without referring to the author as Paul. Some chose to refer to the author as the "Pastor." In most cases, this commentary will refer to the unknown author as simply "the author." At other times, it will be necessary to say, "The author, speaking as Paul," since the author has taken some events from Paul's life and inserted them in such a way that Pauline authorship seems extremely authentic.

Some modern commentators believe that the author used Paul's name to refute others who were using his name to propose false teachings. Since many of the people were unable to read Paul's letters, some preachers could preach messages contrary to those taught by Paul and convince their audience that Paul had indeed written such messages. With an emerging organization of bishops and presbyters in the Church, it was necessary to present a proper message of a structure which sought to faithfully preserve its apostolic tradition. The Pastoral Letters sought to present such a message.

There are many reasons for most scholars to doubt the Pauline authorship. The style of Paul's letters was often strong, direct, and emotional, whereas the pastoral letters are more specific and far less emotional. The most convincing argument against Pauline authorship is the situation of the Church that is addressed in the pastorals. The content reveals a Church far more advanced and organized than that found in Paul's time, with bishops, elders, and deacons having specific functions. The vocabulary differs to a great extent from that used in Paul's other letters, and some words actually have different meanings from those found in Paul's writings. The institutional aspects addressed in these letters appear to be a second-century development within the Church.

As the Church developed, false and subtle teachings were beginning to challenge the doctrines of the Church. Many commentators believed that the main heresy that threatened the Church when the letter was written was a heresy known as Gnosticism, which claimed to have secret knowledge about the mysteries of God's relationship with the world. Gnosticism, however, included many factions which often did not agree with one another. This makes it difficult to identify Gnosticism as a single, consistent form of teaching. Since little is known about this heresy, it becomes difficult for some to claim that the Pastoral Letters were specifically combating this or that particular heresy, although there are apparently some aspects of Gnostic teachings challenged in the pastorals.

Outline for 1 Timothy

Greeting, Prayer, and Order in Ministry (1:1—3:16)

The letter receives its name from the person the author addresses as Timothy, who was Paul's companion. The first part urges Timothy to instruct some unnamed people not to teach false doctrines. The author views Timothy as one sent by the community to fight against false teachings. The author speaks of God as savior. Although the author speaks of worship within the Church, he is actually looking at the Church at prayer as it relates to the world around it. He elaborates about the qualities of bishops and deacons and ends the passage with an ancient hymn about Christ.

Order in the Church (4:1—6:21)

The author warns against false asceticism, noting that everything created by God is good. He urges Timothy to train himself in true doctrine and to ignore those who have contempt for him because of his youth. He establishes rules for the treatment of elders, widows, presbyters, and slaves. One should be content with food and clothing and to avoid the sins of the rich. The author urges Timothy to tell the rich to rely on God rather than on their wealth.

Outline for 2 Timothy

Witnessing to the Lord (1:1—2:26)

The author begins with the usual greeting and thanksgiving. In Paul's name, he offers himself as a model for Timothy to follow, reminding Timothy about the gifts the Lord has given to him, especially the gift of true faith. He urges Timothy to remain faithful to the message he has learned and to recognize that suffering will accompany those who preach the message of Christ. He stresses the need for Timothy to join others in pursuing faith, love, and peace with a pure heart and encourages him to correct others so that they will return to faith in the Lord.

Faithfulness to the Message (3:1—4:22)

The author gives an example of the vices of false teachers and urges Timothy to remain faithful to what he has learned. He must preach this message at all times, both when convenient and inconvenient. The author, speaking as Paul, relays his own example of faithfully serving the Lord, and offers his ministry as a model for Timothy. He speaks as though he is coming to the end of his life, saying that he has finished the race and kept the faith.

In the midst of his instructions to Timothy, Paul expresses his own loneliness and longing for Timothy to join him.

The Letter to Titus

The Letter to Titus consists of only three chapters. Titus was a Gentile convert and coworker with Paul during his third missionary journey. He apparently came from Antioch (Galatians 2:1) and was later sent to Corinth when the community was undergoing one of the many crises it faced in the early years of its development (2 Corinthians 7:13–15). Titus had the duty of taking up the collection at Corinth to be used for the needs of the Church at Jerusalem. The present letter places him as an administrator of the Christian community at Crete.

In the Letter to Titus, the author tells Titus to choose elders for the Christian community at Crete, and he provides a list of qualifications for elders and bishops. He tells Titus to offer counsel to people of every age, and he urges Christians to accept the control of civic authority.

THE LETTER TO THE HEBREWS

Hebrew Background

In the Letter to the Hebrews, the author compares the priesthood of Jesus with the priesthood of the high priests of the Old Testament period. Understanding the background of the priesthood of the Old Testament will be helpful in understanding the Letter to the Hebrews.

Abraham was the father of Isaac, and Isaac was the father of Jacob, who was the father of the twelve sons of Israel. Among the sons was one named Levi, whose offspring were later chosen by the Lord during the Israelites' journey through the desert to be priests for the Israelite nation. This right to priesthood belonged only to the offspring of Levi.

Moses and Aaron belonged to the line of Levi, but during the Israelites' journey through the desert, God directed Moses to set aside Aaron and his sons as priests who would offer sacrifice on behalf of the people. The other offspring of Levi would also serve as priests, but their function would be to care for the implements in the sanctuary and those used for worship.

The Lord told Moses to dress Aaron in special vestments as a sign of Aaron's office as high priest and to perform a ritual anointing and sacrifice on behalf of Aaron. After this, the sons of Aaron were also anointed as priests, but there was to be only one living high priest (see Exodus 28 and 29).

After living separately from the community of the Israelites for seven days after the consecration of Aaron and his sons, Aaron came forward on the eighth day, blessed the people, and with Moses, entered the tabernacle to take possession of it. Taking possession of the tabernacle meant that the sons of Aaron would offer sacrifice in the tabernacle of the Lord, which was the area where the Lord dwelt. During the journey of the Israelites in the desert, the tabernacle was a portable dwelling place. God instructed Moses on the construction of the tabernacle, which contained an inner chamber known as the *Holy of Holies*, and an outer chamber known as the *Holy Place*. The *Holy of Holies* was separated from the outer chamber by a veil.

The priestly family of Levi had the duty of caring for the tent of worship for each tribe. When the Israelites divided the land into twelve units for the twelve tribes of Israel, the tribe of Levi did not receive an allotted piece of land, but received a portion of land within each of the settlements of the twelve tribes. As a result, the offspring of Levi received their call to priesthood, not because they chose it, but because they were born into it. Since the offspring of Aaron were the priests who offered sacrifice at the altar, the role of "high priest" would come from the line of Aaron.

In the desert, when Aaron was nearing death, he, his son (Eleazar), and Moses ascended a mountain where Moses stripped Aaron of his priestly garments and put them on Eleazar, thus designating him as high priest over his brothers. With the death of Aaron, the people accepted Eleazar as their high priest. This passing on of the role of high priest would continue as each high priest died. The author of the Letter to the Hebrews will refer to this need to choose a new high priest in Israel at the death of the previous high priest.

The author of the letter apparently encountered an audience weary of living as Christians in the midst of pagans, and he recognized the need to inspire them with solid theology. He chose to teach a deep, theological truth, encouraging his readers to trust Jesus Christ and recognize how he changed their lives. He teaches that Jesus Christ is the one and only eternal high priest of the New Covenant, the one who offered his life as a sacrifice for our salvation. He tells us that we all share in the eternal priesthood of Jesus Christ who calls us his brothers and sisters.

Author

In the early centuries, some believed that Paul wrote the Letter to the Hebrews, and this belief apparently helped it to become so well received. During the last five centuries, a large number of commentators rejected the idea of Pauline authorship. Although the author appears to be familiar with some of Paul's letters, the style, language, and theology have no resemblance to any characteristics found in the letters of Paul.

Origen, a third-century theologian, attributed the letter to an unknown author. Because of the excellent Greek and the exalted style of the writing, some commentators suspect that Apollos, a companion of Paul who was noted for his oratorical skills, is the true author of the Letter to the Hebrews. Commentators named other members of the early Church community as possible authors of the letter, but lacking solid proof, the list of names is only a guess. In the end, we must simply state that the Letter to the Hebrews was written by an anonymous author.

Characteristics of the Letter

Except for the ending, the Letter to the Hebrews neither sounds like a letter nor follows a letter format. Instead, it resembles a long sermon that presents an explanation of the Old Covenant and its relationship to Christ. It exhorts the community to remain firm in faith and hope. The author writes in excellent Greek and uses as a source the Septuagint, a Greek translation of the Old Testament.

Date and Place

Some commentators date the writing of this sermon near the end of the first century, based mainly on a letter from Clement of Rome, who wrote around the year 96 AD. In the First Letter of Clement of Rome, Clement uses statements that sound as though they originated in the Letter to the Hebrews. Although Clement may be quoting from Hebrews, he could be using a source also used by the Hebrews author even though Clement does not claim to be quoting from Hebrews. The internal evidence in the sermon seems to support the idea that it was written somewhere within the second half of the first century. This could be anywhere from 60 to 90 AD.

Due to the references referring to Temple worship, some commentators believe that the author wrote Hebrews before the Temple was destroyed around 70 AD. The author, however, may not have viewed the destruction of the Temple as significant for his message. Although the author speaks of activities that usually took place in the Temple (sacrifice and forms of offerings), he may simply be knowledgeable about Old Testament writings, which not only viewed the Temple as a place of worship but also saw the tent or tabernacle in the wilderness as the place of worship during the sojourn in the desert.

The closing of the letter contains greetings from "those from Italy" (13:24), which may support the theory that the Letter to the Hebrews was actually written in Rome. Most commentators, however, do not view this supposition as convincing.

Audience

Although the present title of the letter is "The Letter to the Hebrews," this greeting is found nowhere in the letter. In the past, some commentators believed that the continual reference to the Old Testament showed that it was written to a Jewish audience who would naturally be concerned with the Old Testament. Most commentators today, however, believe that it was written to Christians, both Jewish and Greek, who were familiar with the Greek Old Testament. Toward the end of the first century, Greek

Christians would have realized the importance of the Old Testament to the Christian message.

Outline of the Letter to the Hebrews

The Theme of the Letter and the Identity of Jesus Christ (1:1—4:13)

The opening of the letter speaks immediately about Christ's exalted position as God's Son and his special place above that of the angels. Since Christ is so exalted and since he has become human for our sake, we are urged to pay special attention to his message. Christ is more exalted than Moses, and we should avoid hardening our heart against the message of God as the people of Israel did in the desert. The Word of God which comes through Christ is like a two-edged sword that cuts deeply into our life.

The Accomplishments of Jesus Christ (4:14—10:18)

The author describes how Christ qualifies to become a high priest, but a high priest of the New Covenant. After exhorting his listeners to pay attention to the basics of Christ's message and to move on from there, the author shows how Christ belongs to the eternal priesthood of Melchizedek rather than to the temporal priesthood of Levi. As the new high priest of the New Covenant, Christ offers himself once and for all for our salvation. In Christ, the Old Covenant gives way to the new.

Encouragement in the Faith and the Ending of the Letter (10:19—13:25)

The author contrasts the limitations of the Old Covenant with the gifts of the New Covenant, and he uses this as a reason for his listeners to remain faithful to what they have heard. He chooses magnificent examples from the heroes of the past (the Old Testament) and calls his listeners to live their lives in union with Christ, who never changes. Christians should keep their eyes on Christ. They are to enter the new tabernacle, the heavenly Jerusalem, through him. More explicitly, the author tells his readers how they should live a life worthy of their calling.

Authentic Teaching

1 TIMOTHY 1–3

For there is one God. There is also one mediator between God and the human race, Christ Jesus, himself human, who gave himself as ransom for all (2:5–6).

Opening Prayer (SEE PAGE 18)

Context

The author writes his letter to Timothy, whom he calls his child in faith. He sends the letter to Timothy to alert him to the need for proper teaching of the faith against the false teachings the people were being taught. He expresses his gratitude to the Lord for appointing him to his ministry of preaching about Christ. Looking to his past grievances against Christianity, which he attributes to his ignorance, he proclaims that the Lord has treated him with compassion and mercy. He entrusts to Timothy to following the directions the author is about to give him, knowing Timothy will have to endure hardship. He urges Timothy and those whom he will teach to pray for all, for kings and all in authority, based on the belief there is one God and one mediator of the human race, namely Jesus Christ. He then teaches proper decorum for women in worship and society.

GROUP STUDY (1 TIMOTHY 1—2)

Read aloud 1 Timothy 1—2.

1:1–2 Greeting

The letter begins with a typical greeting found in the letters of Paul. Since the author writes as though he is Paul and shows signs of being well aware of Paul's mind and message, this text will use the name Paul as though he is the actual author of the letter. In the letters accepted as having been written by Paul, he begins by referring to himself as an apostle. The author does the same in this letter to Timothy.

Paul bases his authority on his role as an apostle of Christ Jesus. This authority did not come to him because he sought it, but it came as a result of God's will. Shortly after Paul's conversion, Ananias, a disciple in the early Church, received a message from the Lord, who told him Paul was a chosen instrument to carry the Lord's name before Gentiles, kings, and Israelites (see Acts of the Apostles 9:15). During his lifetime, Paul had to defend his right to apostleship, since he was not one of the original apostles who traveled with Jesus, but one called to be an apostle after his conversion to Christ.

The author refers to God as "our savior." In Paul's letters, Paul occasionally refers to Christ as our savior (see Philippians 3:20), but does not use this expression for God the Father. Paul may be using God as our savior to contrast the Christian belief about God with false teachings concerning other types of so-called saviors. He then calls Christ Jesus "our hope," recalling that Jesus—and no one else—is the hope of Christianity.

The letter is addressed to Timothy. In the Acts of the Apostles 16:1, the author tells us that Timothy, the son of a Jewish mother and a Greek father, was Paul's constant companion from the time of his second missionary journey onwards. Because Timothy's father did not believe in the need for religious circumcision, Paul had to have Timothy circumcised so he could preach to the Jews. As the one who brought Timothy to faith in Christ, Paul addresses Timothy as his loyal child in the faith.

The greeting ends with the usual wish that the recipients share in grace and peace, but the author adds the word *mercy*, which expresses God's loving generosity for all people. This greeting is given in the typical Christian fashion, that is, in the name of "God the Father and Christ Jesus our Lord." By referring to Christ Jesus as "Lord," Paul is expressing his faith in Christ as one with God the Father.

1:3–11 Warning Against False Doctrine

Paul seeks to correct errors arising from those who lack a true understanding of the faith. He implies he has already spoken to Timothy about his mission, reminding him of the directives he gave him on the way to Macedonia. On this journey, Paul the Apostle urged Timothy and others to teach the truth, knowing that savage wolves, i.e., those who would devour the truth, will come among them and not spare the flock, i.e., they will teach false doctrines (Acts 20:17–38).

The Pastor tells Timothy to remain at Ephesus with a twofold task. First, he is to warn the people of the area against teaching any doctrines that differ from those taught by Paul; second, he must stop the people from occupying themselves with useless speculation concerning myths and genealogies, and encourage them to train themselves in the faith.

In his letter, Paul speaks of false teachings and idle speculations, but commentators are not able to identify these specific heresies. When he speaks of training in the faith, he is speaking about learning the doctrines of the faith and living them. In this letter, faith means much more than belief. It also involves the need to be nourished by knowledge. In contrast to the desires of the people and the world of false teachers, the author reminds Timothy that this requirement for training in the faith comes from God. He is to lead Christians to practice virtues that clearly identify them as followers of Christ. Christ's followers should have a love that comes from a heart that is pure, and a conscience formed by a sincere faith. Some have rejected these virtues and turned to empty talk. They wish to be teachers, but they do not understand what they are talking about, discussing false matters with a bogus assurance.

Paul states the law is established, not for the innocent, but for sinful people. The list of vices he presents in this letter is one of several lists found in the early teachings of the Church. The law is given for those who live without any reference to the law, those who are disobedient, godless and sinful, unholy and ungodly; who kill their father or mother, murderers, fornicators, sodomites, slave traders, liars, perjurers, and whatever else is contrary to sound teaching. Sound teaching includes the Gospel of God which has been entrusted to Paul.

1:12–20 Gratitude for God's Mercy

In Paul's letters, a thanksgiving usually follows the greeting, and he ordinarily thanks God for the faithfulness of the community being addressed. In this letter, he places his thanksgiving after his greeting and statement of purpose. Since the Lord judged him as faithful to the message and appointed him to be of service to the Lord, Paul thanks Christ Jesus for strengthening him to serve.

Paul recalls his past sinfulness and accuses himself as being a blasphemer, a persecutor, and an arrogant person. This is a reference to the life of Paul before his conversion. During that time, he was a dedicated Jew who persecuted those who preached the message of Christ. God treated him in a merciful manner, because he acted out of ignorance. Referring to his conversion on the road to Damascus, Paul declares the Lord has showered him with an abundance of graces.

Because his message is based on his proven truthfulness and faith, the author, speaking as Paul, asserts that Timothy can be open to his message even before Timothy hears it. This is in contrast to the messages of false teachers which cannot be accepted. Paul states that Christ Jesus came into the world to save sinners, and he considers himself to be among the worst because of his persecution of Christians. Jesus Christ, however, is displaying extreme patience with him, treating him with mercy and giving an example to others who would come to believe in Christ for eternal life.

Paul suddenly bursts into praise of God, calling God "the King of the ages, immortal, invisible, the only God" (1:17). This outburst not only praises God, but may also have served as an example of praise for the true

God in contrast to some of the false teachings about God being taught to the people. One heresy of the day was that there was a good God and an evil God. Paul praises the Lord with a Jewish prayer of praise for the Lord.

As he did in an earlier passage, Paul repeats that he is going to give Timothy certain instructions. The first set of directions was more general, while this set will be more specific. The directions will be in line with the prophecies that earlier pointed to Timothy. Later in this same letter (4:14), we will read that the presbyters laid hands on Timothy as a result of prophecy. In the Acts of the Apostles, the Spirit directed the community at Antioch to set aside Barnabas and Saul for the work the Lord gave them to do. The community fasted and prayed and laid hands on them (see Acts 13:2). This passage in Acts was considered a result of prophecy, akin to the same expression used in this letter concerning Timothy, who is set aside for his ministry. In the Early Church, leaders were chosen by the community.

In giving these directions, Paul tells Timothy he is preparing him to fight with confidence. The imagery of entering the battle of good against evil occurs often in Paul's letters. Inspired by these prophecies and the laying on of hands, Timothy will be able to wage war against the enemy and remain firm in faith and in good conscience.

The author names two men who rejected the guidance of their consciences and suffered shipwreck in the faith. These men are both mentioned later in the Second Letter to Timothy. Hymenaeus caused confusion by declaring a person's resurrection had already taken place (2 Timothy 2:17–18), and Alexander, a coppersmith, caused harm for Paul (2 Timothy 4:14). Paul informs Timothy that he has turned these two men over to Satan in order to teach them not to blaspheme. The author is stating that Hymenaeus and Alexander were excommunicated, not for the sake of abandoning them, but for the sake of their repentance.

2:1–7 Prayer and Conduct

In this passage, Paul recognizes that the Church exists in a world populated with people who lack faith in Christ, but whose lives closely touch the lives of Christians. He emphasizes the need for the Church to pray for everyone, for kings and all who are in high positions. The reason given for such prayer is to assure that the members of the Church are to live quiet and peaceable lives in holiness and dignity. Prayer for a ruler could convince that ruler the Church is not a threat to his authority. Not only will prayer for these rulers bring about a free and peaceful atmosphere for the practice of the faith, but it will also be pleasing to God, who wishes all people to be saved and to come to the knowledge of the truth.

The truth, for Paul, is that "there is one God" and that "Christ Jesus... who gave himself as ransom for all," is the "one mediator between God and the human race" (2:5). The pagans prayed to the emperor and kings as gods. Paul urges Christians not to pray *to* these false gods, but to pray *for* them. Unlike the pagans, who saw their rulers as mediators between the gods and people, Christians see Jesus Christ as the one mediator between the one God and human beings. Jesus' death on the cross was a ransom paid for all people, not only for Christians. This idea of paying the ransom does not infer that someone else possessed the world before Jesus died on the cross. Paul does not mention anyone who is to receive this ransom. He views himself as an apostle to all nations, as the one chosen by God to teach the truth of the Gospel message.

2:8–15 Rules for Women

The author expresses his desire that all people should offer prayers with their hands symbolically held high, without anger or disagreements. Many commentators view this way of offering prayers in such a manner as making the whole passage pertain to worship.

The author then speaks about the role of women, offering comments which reflect the unchallenged cultural conditioning of the time. The comments could also be the author's rejection of the practices of the Gentile pagans who sometimes placed women in a leadership role. The author teaches that women should dress in a modest and decent fashion; they should not decorate themselves with braided hair, gold, pearls, or expensive clothing, but instead should adorn themselves with their good works to show reverence for God. They should learn in silence and with respect, not teaching or having authority over a man.

In writing about the role of women, the author of the letter seems to forget that Paul, in his letters, speaks of women who are prophets and deaconesses. As a source for the teaching presented here, the author refers to the Book of Genesis and interprets the story of Adam and Eve as a sign of a man's authority over a woman. He reminds them that Adam was created first and that Eve was the first to sin. Although a better understanding would be that sin entered the world through men and women collectively, the author ignores this tradition and supports his message, concluding that women can redeem themselves by performing those deeds for which they were created, namely, "through motherhood,...faith and love and holiness, with self-control" (2:15). In the author's culture, the woman's role was primarily the rearing of children and the care of the home.

Review Questions

1. Who is Timothy?
2. Why does the author, speaking as Paul, consider the Lord has treated him mercifully?
3. Why was it important for Timothy to teach the message of Jesus correctly?
4. Why is the author concerned about praying for kings and emperors?
5. What do you think about the author's regulations regarding women?

Closing Prayer (SEE PAGE 18)

Pray the closing prayer now or after *lectio divina*.

Lectio Divina (SEE PAGE 11)

Relax your body and maintain a posture of prayer (back straight, eyes shut, feet flat on the floor). This exercise can take as long as you want, but in the context of this Bible study, ten to twenty minutes should be sufficient.

The meditations that follow are provided only to help group participants use this prayer form, but note that *lectio* is intended to bring one to a place of prayerful contemplation where the Word of God speaks to the hearer from his or her heart. (See page 11 for further instruction.)

Greeting (1:1–2)

The author, speaking as Paul, reflects the affection Paul had for Timothy. He is about to give Timothy the difficult task of correcting false doctrines and confronting those proposing these doctrines. He wishes him grace, mercy, and peace from the Lord, while knowing that Timothy will have to face some difficult times ahead. The call of Timothy reflects the call many Christians must face.

As Christians, we receive the call of bringing the message of Christ into a world that often ignores Christ's message or totally rejects it. The love of Christ calls us, but the call, as wonderful as it is, leaves us with an extremely difficult and, in some cases, dangerous mission. The love of Christ called the martyrs and saints to serve, but the task would demand great courage and faithfulness from them. Someone once said it is easier to die for Christ than to live for Christ. As Christians, we have received the call to live for Christ and to make Christ's presence visible to the world by the way we live our life—a truly challenging task.

✠ *What can I learn from this passage?*

Warning Against False Doctrine (1:3–11)

Timothy lived in a world where many false teachers spoke with a sense of authority, making Jesus' message fit their own attitudes toward life. A movie star on television said that he felt no need to belong to a particular religion and he prayed alone as Jesus always did. The reality is Jesus was a regular churchgoer as we read in Luke's Gospel. Luke tells us Jesus "went according to his custom into the synagogue on the sabbath day" (Luke 4:16). In the world today, we see some movie stars on television giving their own interpretations of what is right and what is wrong. They speak with an air of authority on moral issues and issues about the existence of God. In many cases, they are justifying their own attitude toward life and sometimes rationalize away the message of Jesus.

There are many good Christian movie stars who have learned about Jesus and remain faithful to his message, but we know there are others who tell us what they think with little knowledge about Jesus' message.

They become their own messiahs. The world has not changed that much since the author of Timothy wrote his letter.

✠ *What can I learn from this passage?*

Gratitude for God's Mercy (1: 12–20)

Jesus told his disciples they should not judge in order to avoid being judged themselves, inferring that they will have to face the form of judgment they impose on others. In reality, none of us has the ability and insight to judge the condition of the soul of another. Jesus also said much is expected of those to whom much has been given. In the early life of Paul the apostle, he became so zealous for the Mosaic Law that he believed he had to persecute those Jews who dared to reject the law or impose the message of Christ on other Jews. Paul's conversion to Christ, however, made him realize he had judged God's intent for creation falsely. Those whom Paul judged to be sinners were actually spreading the message of love as given by Jesus.

Paul considered himself the worst of sinners because of his persecution of the followers of Jesus, and he adds to his confession a message about a loving and forgiving God. He realized the Lord was willing to bless him because the Lord recognized that he was acting out of ignorance. The message Paul leaves with us is no matter how badly we have sinned in the past, the loving God is always ready to forgive us. Because God is a forgiving God who looks into our heart and knows the motive behind our actions, we can never determine how God is judging us or others who may not have received the graces we have received. The message encourages us to leave judgment up to God and to live as closely to the Lord as we can.

✠ *What can I learn from this passage?*

Prayer and Conduct (2:1–7)

A monk once decided to send a group of four monks to a foreign country where the people who lived there did not believe in God. The people would recognize these monks in robes as they lived among them and shopped each day. While they shopped, they would take time to speak with the people about the weather, their children, and matters of daily concern in their lives, but they never mentioned Christ to them.

Each day, however, the people of the town would hear a hand bell sound at six in the morning, noon, and at six in the evening, and they would watch as the monks gathered in a garden outside their house to pray. One by one, the people came to the monks to ask them about the faith that made them so dedicated to prayer, and one by one, many of the people of the area converted to Christianity.

Like the Christians for whom the author is writing, we are living in a world where we rub shoulders with people who do not believe in Christ or in God. We live in a secular society that often makes decisions which are contrary to the message of Jesus. The author of Timothy speaks about rubbing shoulders with unbelievers, and he tells the people to pray for all people and for the civil leaders, whether or not they have the same beliefs as the followers of Christ. This need to pray for our leaders is for the common good of a society. We can pray they follow moral standards that agree with those given to us by Christ, and we can pray that their decisions are always just and fair. In doing this, Christians are following the directives of Christ, who said we are called to be in the world but not of the world, which means our first allegiance is always to God, no matter how secular our society becomes.

✠ *What can I learn from this passage?*

Rules for Women (2:8–15)

Although Paul received an insight into the message of Jesus, he was also shaped by his own era and culture concerning the place of women in society and worship. The author's strict words concerning decorum for women should not be taken as revelation, but as a statement of the common thinking of the day.

In the United States before 1920, women did not have the right to vote in national elections, and many men and women believed it was not logical for women to be able to vote. Some American theologians even believed it was against the natural law for women to vote, since the woman's place was in the home. If Paul wrote in 1900, he might have stated women should not have the right to vote, since it was contrary to the role of women in society. Today we recognize the importance of women voting in our elections. In our society, we have women in the workplace and women who decide to work within the home. Both forms of life are highly respected.

✠ *What can I learn from this passage?*

Proper Conduct

1 TIMOTHY 3—6

But if I should be delayed, you should know how to behave in the household of God, which is the church of the living God, the pillar and foundation of truth (3:15).

Opening Prayer (SEE PAGE 18)

Context

Part 1: 1 Timothy 3—4 The author establishes the qualifications to be found in the selection of bishops and deacons. He writes about these qualifications to tell the people how to behave in the household of God. If they cannot manage their own household, how will they manage "the household of God, which," he states, "is the church of the living God" (3:15)? The author warns against false asceticism which forbids marriage and the eating of certain kinds of food, stating that everything God created is good. After speaking about false asceticism, he instructs Timothy to train himself spiritually and to teach the truth in order to be a good minister of Jesus Christ. Although he is young, he is to set an example of living his message for the people to follow.

Part 2: 1 Timothy 5—6 The author writes about Timothy's duties toward others, including his duties toward the elderly, widows, presbyters, and slaves. He confronts the false teachings of those who are preaching something different from the message he gave to Timothy, and he warns against temptations in striving for wealth. Timothy should strive to keep the commandments and urge the rich not to rely on uncertain wealth, but to rely on the treasures of their good works.

PART 1: GROUP STUDY (1 TIMOTHY 3—4)

Read aloud 1 Timothy 3—4.

3:1–7 Qualifications for Bishops

The author begins by stating that he is instructing the community with certainty when he tells them about the qualifications for bishop. The word *bishop* does not refer to bishops as we know them today, but rather to leaders of the community, known as the overseers of the community. Because the role of leadership is important·to the community, the author lists personal virtues the bishop must possess, and he then follows with external signs that refer to the bishop's family, position in the Church, and relationship to those outside the Church.

The bishop must be a man above reproach, "married only once," sensible, respectable, hospitable, a good teacher, gentle, peaceful, and moderate in his use of drink and money (3:2–3). His management of his own household is an indication of how successfully he will lead others. This elder must show signs of managing his household well, and his children should be respectful and obedient. To avoid any pride that could lead him into sin, the bishop must not be a new convert. He must also be held in esteem by those outside the Church, so that he does not fall into disgrace and into the trap of the devil. This last qualification reveals the author's concern for the proper place of the Christian in the pagan world.

3:8–16 Qualifications for Deacons

The author turns his attention to the deacon. The role of the deacon is not clearly indicated, but the qualifications are as strict as those needed for anyone who strives to be an elder or overseer (bishop) of a community. In the Acts of the Apostles, we read that deacons were appointed to care for the Greek widows (see Acts 6:1–4), but their duty also extended to preaching the Word of God (6:8–10; 8:4–6). The First Letter to Timothy adds other stipulations. Deacons must be serious, direct, and truthful, moderate in their drink, and not greedy for any personal gain. They must hold onto the faith with a clear conscience. In the pagan world, those seeking an office had to undergo a period of testing first. The author believes that the same type of testing period should apply to those seeking to be a deacon. This period refers to the manner in which one responds to the call of being a Christian in the world. Only if nothing is found against them may they serve as deacons.

The author interrupts his message with an abrupt statement about the role of women. He says that women must also be serious and trustworthy, "not slanderers, but temperate and faithful in everything" (3:11). Although the author may be addressing the wives of deacons here, most commentators believe he is speaking to deaconesses.

Like those chosen as bishops, the deacons must be married no more than one time, and should be good managers of their children and households. If they serve well, they will receive a place of high standing for themselves and gain assurance in their works for Christ Jesus. The author seems to be saying that deacons should find their ministry to be a rewarding experience that strengthens their faith.

In his letters, Paul often expresses his desire to visit the community to whom he is writing. Paul does the same here. In the event that his visit is delayed, he tells them that he is writing to them so they may know how to conduct themselves as members of the household of God, which he identifies as "the church of the living God, the pillar and foundation of truth" (3:15).

As the firm foundation of all truth, the Church knows the mystery of God's plan, which it professes with a living faith. The author quotes part of an early Christian hymn to profess this mystery that was revealed through Jesus' life on earth. He was revealed in flesh and vindicated in spirit, meaning that Jesus was put to death and raised from the dead. His resurrection was announced by the angels, and preached to the Gentiles. People throughout the world believed in him, and he was taken up in glory. Implied in this last idea is the message that Jesus is Lord and will come again.

4:1–5 False Asceticism

The author states the Spirit warned that false teachers would arise, who will themselves turn away from the faith and strive to lead others away from the truth with false ascetical practices. What they teach will sound logical, but, in reality, they will be teaching the message of fraudulent spirits and demons. Perhaps prompted by the image of branded fugitive slaves, the author describes these false teachers, now enslaved by evil, as liars "with branded consciences" (4:2).

False teachers forbid marriage and the eating of certain foods. They urge a withdrawal from the material world, which they view as evil—a perspective found in Gnosticism and other heretical beliefs. The author does not accept this thinking, stating that everything God created is good. Nothing created by God is to be rejected, provided it is received with a spirit of thanksgiving. Abstaining from food does not make a person holy. God's Word and the prayer of the people sanctify creation.

4:6–16 Timothy's Example

The author tells Timothy that he will be a good minister and servant of Christ to the brothers and sisters in the Church if he passes on the instructions he received from Paul. He will be nourished by the words of faith and sound teaching that he (Timothy) has already been following. The author warns Timothy to avoid worldly myths, and he further tells him to train himself spiritually, adding that, as valuable as physical training is, it is limited. Devotion is valuable in every way because it offers a promise of life now and life hereafter. He states his message is true and worthy of full acceptance. The author reminds Timothy that all followers of Christ toil and struggle because they have placed all their hope in the living God, whom he identifies for the second time in his letter as the savior of all, especially believers.

As a faithful follower of Christ, Timothy must urge the people to follow his message.

In Timothy's day, old age was respected as a time when a person had wisdom which was gained from a lifetime of experiences, and youth was a time when people should listen to their elders. The author tells Timothy not to allow the people to look down on him because of his youth, but to set an example "in speech, conduct, love, faith, and purity" (4:12). Timothy's mission as set forth here is to continue to read the scriptures to the people, to preach, and to teach them until Paul arrives. He is directed not to neglect the gift he received through prophecy with the laying on of hands by the council of elders. The prophecy alludes to the manner in which Timothy was chosen to preside over the community. The call to leadership was fulfilled when the leaders of the community laid hands on him.

Because of his special call, Timothy must pay attention to his duties and devote himself totally to them so that everyone will be able to witness his progress. By attending to himself and the teachings he received from Paul, Timothy will save himself and those who listen to him.

Review Questions

1. What are your thoughts about the manner of life demanded of bishops in 1 Timothy?
2. What are your thoughts about the manner of life demanded of deacons in 1 Timothy?
3. Why does the author reject some forms of asceticism?
4. What is the meaning behind the laying on of hands on Timothy?

Closing Prayer (SEE PAGE 18)

Pray the closing prayer now or after *lectio divina*.

Lectio Divina (SEE PAGE 11)

Relax your body and maintain a posture of prayer (back straight, eyes shut, feet flat on the floor). This exercise can take as long as you want, but in the context of this Bible study, ten to twenty minutes should be sufficient.

The meditations that follow are provided only to help group participants use this prayer form, but note that *lectio* is intended to bring one to a place of prayerful contemplation where the Word of God speaks to the hearer from his or her heart. (See page 11 for further instruction.)

Qualifications for Bishops (3:1–7)

When a particular diocese was expecting an appointment of a new bishop, some ordained priests and laity sent notes to those in charge of naming a bishop, outlining the qualities they hoped to find in their new bishop. Except for the qualification of being married only once and controlling his children (qualifications they ignored), they sent the list of qualifications similar to those found in the First Letter to Timothy. Some people laughed when they saw the qualifications found in these letters, asking if there were anyone who could fit all these demands. It seemed that the people were seeking a superhuman person.

The author of the First Letter to Timothy recognized the dedication needed for a person to be a leader in the Church, and he believed that people of such high virtue did indeed exist. In reality, these qualifications should be the aim of all people who profess to be followers of Christ.

✠ *What can I learn from this passage?*

Qualifications for Deacons (3:8–16)

The author's qualifications for deacons parallel those of bishops. Bishops and deacons who live exemplary lives represent the Church and become an example for other members of the Church. For the Church to remain faithful to Christ, it must have leaders who faithfully live Jesus' message. The hope the author exhibits is that the Church will learn to live Christ's message not only through the preaching of its leaders and guides, but through their example. Someone once said, "What you are shouts so loudly that I can't hear what you are saying." The daily lives of Church leaders and guides are to shout out to the world their love for Christ. Once a person accepts a specific role in the Church, that person has the obligation to live as an exemplary Christian in the world.

✠ *What can I learn from this passage?*

False Asceticism (4:1–5)

In the early days of the Church, many hermits went into the desert to live a highly ascetical life, which included eating a sparse amount of food and ceaselessly praying. Saint Anthony of the desert chose this form of life, and others went into the desert to learn from him. In time, ascetics went beyond the practices of St. Anthony and crucified their body with practices of fasting and self-beatings to the point that, within a short period of time, they became ill. The need for a change of attitude was obvious.

Saint Benedict saw what was happening to many of those who chose lives as hermits, and he wrote a rule which called for a balanced approach to asceticism, one that balanced prayer, work, and fasting in a healthy manner that did not lead to illness or an early death. His monks lived together in a community and supported one another. He taught that true asceticism does not view God's creation as evil, but as a creation that makes the proper use of the gifts of God.

God gave people the ability to work and pray. Saint Benedict's message fits all Christians who live in the world today. We are all called to work and pray in a balanced manner for the sake of the special mission God has given to us. In doing this, we are serving the Lord, no matter where we are.

✠ *What can I learn from this passage?*

Timothy's Example (4:6–16)

A reality of life is that people cannot give what they do not have. For instance, a man who knows nothing about the engine of a car cannot teach another man how to fix a car's engine. When the author writes to Timothy, he encourages Timothy to become a living example of the lesson he teaches. One chosen to the awesome task of teaching the faith must be willing to be a living example of the faith. In order to do this, Timothy must first live a life dedicated to the Lord. He cannot teach true spirituality unless he himself is a spiritual person dedicated to the Lord. The people will more readily accept Timothy's message if they see the message has an influence on his life. All Christians have the awesome task of developing a deep, spiritual relationship with the Lord and teaching the faith through their manner of life.

✠ *What can I learn from this passage?*

PART 2: INDIVIDUAL STUDY (1 TIMOTHY 5—6)

Day 1: Duties Toward Others (1 Timothy 5:1–16)

Despite his leadership role, Timothy must continue to show concern for the elders in the community. He must never speak harshly to an older man, but should speak to him as he would to a father. He should treat younger men as brothers, older women as mothers, and younger women, in a pure manner, as sisters. The leadership to which Timothy is called is not one of lording it over others, but one of treating others with respect.

The author now turns his attention to widows and their place in the household of the Church. He states that all people should have consideration for widows, especially for those he calls "truly widows." He explains that one who is truly a widow is one who has no one to care for her, while a widow with children or grandchildren should be cared for by her family. The children or grandchildren have a debt to pay to their parents, and the care they give them is pleasing to God.

The true widow is a woman who has no one to rely on for support. Having set her sights on God, she spends all of her days and nights in petitions and prayers. The widow, however, who thinks only of fulfilling her own pleasures has already died, although she still physically lives. The author urges Timothy to teach this message so that his listeners may be above reproach. Those who do not look after their relatives, especially members of their immediate families, have denied the faith because their actions show a lack of faith. Such people are worse than pagan unbelievers, since they claim to have faith.

The early Church developed the institution of enrolling widows who chose to dedicate themselves to God and who were supported by the community. The author, however, takes human nature into account, stating that no one should enroll as a widow in the Church unless she is at least sixty years old. Like the bishop and the deacon, the widow must be married only once. She must be a woman of good works, one who has brought up children, shown herself to be hospitable, washed the feet of the saints, helped the afflicted, and devoted herself to doing good. Washing the feet of the saints refers to the practice of washing the feet of a traveler who enters one's house. In describing the widows' service to the local church, the author recalls the example of Christ's washing his disciples' feet as set forth in John 13.

The author warns against enrolling younger widows who might eventually be tempted to marry. Instead of leading to holiness, their enrollment will become a means of condemnation for having violated their commitment. The author shows a lack of trust in a younger woman's ability to keep herself busy. Whereas older women can dedicate themselves to prayer and good works, he views younger women as living a life of leisure, with no family to care for, moving from one house to another, wasting time, and becoming gossips and busybodies. In a previous passage, the author warned Timothy not to forbid marriage as the false teachers do. He now encourages young widows to marry, have children, care for a home, and not give the enemy any reason for speaking against Christians. He states that some women have already sinned by turning away from their commitment and caused scandal.

The author concludes by speaking of the duty of the female members of the Church to care for widowed relatives. He apparently is speaking of the obligation to care for widowed family members, no matter how distant the relationship. The author could also be addressing those who have voluntarily taken on the support of a widow, whether related or not. In both instances, the burden on the local church is decreased, which allows for better support of the real widows, meaning those who are in dire need with no one to care for them.

Lectio Divina

Spend 8 to 10 minutes in silent contemplation of the following passage:

> When the author writes about caring for widows, he is writing as though it is an obligation and not something that would be nice to do. Christians are meant to accept these obligations to care for those in need when they accept Christianity. Jesus showed love and concern for a widow in the Bible when he raises the only son of a widow to life because he took pity on her (see Luke 7:11–17). He later castigates the scribes who devour the houses of widows, saying that they will receive "a very severe condemnation" (Luke 20:47). He praises a widow who makes a donation of two small coins to the Temple treasury, saying that she has put in more than all the rest, because she gave out of her whole livelihood (see Luke 21:1–4). Christ's concern for widows offers an example for Christians concerning widows.

✠ *What can I learn from this passage?*

Day 2: Rules for Presbyters (1 Timothy 5:17–25)

The author shows the importance of preaching and teaching when he tells Timothy that the elders who rule well should be well paid, especially when they perform these ministries. Although the elders did not have Timothy's authority in the community, they were the ones who laid hands on him at the time of his ordination. Timothy was a bishop and a recognized leader of the community who ministered with the elders and other members of the community. Quoting from the "Scripture," the author reminds Timothy that "the laborer deserves his payment" (Luke 10:7). This quotation supports his message that the elders should not have to concern themselves with physical needs but, instead, should be free to spend their time preaching and teaching.

Quoting the passage about payment from Luke's Gospel and referring to it as "Scripture" shows that by the early second century, some books of the New Testament were already considered to belong to "Scripture." The First Letter to Timothy was written in the early second century, more than fifteen years after Luke wrote his Gospel. When those who wrote in the first century referred to the "scriptures," they referred only to the Hebrew Scriptures (the Old Testament).

The author notes that the elders and presbyters, because of their position within the community, will be the object of criticism. He warns Timothy not to listen to any accusation against the elders unless two or three witnesses support it. If an elder proves sinful, however, Timothy is ordered to rebuke him publicly in order to fill the remaining elders with a fear of sinning. As difficult as these precepts are to fulfill, the author commands Timothy—before God, Christ Jesus, and the angels—to carry out these orders without any prejudice or favoritism. Along with this order, Timothy is told not to ordain anyone until that person has been proved worthy. In every way, Timothy is to avoid becoming an accomplice to the sins of others. The author also warns him to keep himself pure.

In his disagreement with those who advocate abstinence from all worldly indulgence, the author shows personal concern for Timothy by telling him that he should take some wine. He reminds Timothy that his health has not been good, and he urges him for the sake of his health to take wine and to avoid drinking only water. This implies a concern of the author that Timothy and his ministry not suffer because of the false teachings of others concerning worldly indulgence.

The author concludes this passage with some wise insights into life. The sins of some are obvious and demand some action be taken against them, but there are other sins that are not so obvious and will appear only later. The author may be referring either to the Day of Judgment when a person stands before God, or to the inevitable recognition of sin in time. The same situation applies to good works. Good deeds may be recognized immediately or at some future time, but they will be recognized.

Lectio Divina

Spend 8 to 10 minutes in silent contemplation of the following passage:

Paul the apostle spoke of being anxious to be with the Lord, which means that he longs for the day when he will spend eternity with the Lord. He states that he is willing to remain here on earth to continue his mission if it is the will of the Lord and if it will help others. In attempting to strike a balance between making sacrifices for the love of God and one's health, the author teaches that taking care of one's health is more important, since all have a mission in God's creation.

Timothy is important to the community, and the author wishes to assure himself that Timothy will be able to serve well his ministry. In some of the letters of the early followers of Christ, the writers stated they rejoiced when they had to suffer for Christ. Some, however, who were not suffering would perform some painful act that would make them suffer and often become ill. Other early spiritual writers taught that a person does not have to seek suffering. Offering up to God the suffering that comes in the daily living of life can be a greater act of holiness than causing our own form of suffering. Living a healthy life is important for our particular mission in life. Many spiritual writers believe this is God's will for us.

✠ *What can I learn from this passage?*

Day 3: Rules for Slaves (6:1–2)

The author, who begins this passage by speaking of the attitudes of slaves within the Christian household, has no concern about the social structure which allows for slavery, but he seeks to teach Christian slaves how to live as Christians within their particular state. Without making any statement about the condition of slavery in his era, he urges slaves to act with respect for their masters, so the name of God, as well as Christian teachings, may not be brought into disgrace. This directive follows the same line of thinking found at the beginning of this letter—namely, the need to live in peace with the civil government. The author clearly does not wish Christian teachings to cause a revolution within the existing social structure.

Because slaves embrace the same teachings as some of their masters, they must not look down on those masters. Since Christian masters are believers and are therefore beloved, they should be treated with greater respect. Paul the Apostle addressed the relationship of slaves to their Christian masters in his Letter to Philemon as well as in his letters to the Colossians and the Ephesians. The author again reminds Timothy that these are the teachings he must share with others.

Lectio Divina

Spend 8 to 10 minutes in silent contemplation of the following passage:

Slavery was accepted throughout the Roman world. Slaves were often foreigners who were conquered and exiled from their home area into another country. In many cases, slaves would starve to death if they were freed, since they had no way of supporting themselves in this foreign land. The best solution in Paul's era was to develop a mutual respect between slaves and their masters.

The author is not necessarily agreeing with slavery in this passage, but he is concerned about the dignity of the human person in a difficult situation. Many slaves had to suffer at the hands of unjust masters, while others served masters who treated them with respect. The mutual respect between slaves and masters underlines the mutual respect Christians should have for all people. In God's eyes, all people are equal, whether slave or free, and all are deserving of respect.

✠ *What can I learn from this passage?*

Day 4: False Teaching and True Wealth (6:3–21)

The author directs Timothy to teach and urge the people to follow his message. Using strong language, the author attacks those who teach messages contrary to the teachings of Christ and the firm doctrines of true religion, stating that they should be seen as conceited and ignorant with a craving for arguments and for disputes about the use of words. The author's accusation here is clearly hurled against those who claim they are wise because of their intelligent-sounding arguments. Among those who taught this were some Gnostics who believed they possessed secret knowledge which others were unable to understand.

The author warns that these false teachings cause disunity within the community, leading to sins such as envy, dissension, slander, base suspicions, and wrangling among people who lack reason and truth. Such people view religion only as a means of personal gain. The author states that religion does offer gain, but the gain comes with godliness and contentment. He teaches that none of us brought anything into the world, and none of us will take anything out of it. Food and clothing are all we need, and these should leave us content.

Those who are seeking wealth are allowing themselves to be tempted and trapped by senseless and harmful desires that lead only to destruction. The author reminds the reader that "the love of money is the root of all evils" (6:10). The eagerness of some people for wealth led them away from the faith and filled their life with an abundance of pain.

The author reminds Timothy that he is committed to God and, as such, must avoid all the errors of false teachers. He specifically lists the virtues that Timothy must practice: "righteousness, devotion, faith, love, patience, and gentleness" (6:11). Furthermore, Timothy must fight the good fight of the faith to attain as his prize the gift of eternal life to which he was called. This call apparently alludes to a commitment Timothy made before the assembly, possibly at his baptism or at the time of his consecration to ministry.

The author calls on God, the source of all life, and Christ Jesus, who remained a faithful witness to the truth before Pilate, to witness to the charge he is giving Timothy. He orders Timothy to follow the command of God and to carry out—blamelessly and without reproach—everything he has been told, until the Lord, Jesus Christ, appears. This points to the Second Coming of Christ at the end of time and at which time the manifestation of Christ will be made to all people. It is more than a visitation from the Lord; it is a manifestation of the Lord.

This manifestation of the Lord will be brought about by God at the appointed time. He gives praise to God, calling him the "King of kings and the Lord of lords" (6:15). Pagans praised the emperors with these words, but the author adds that Jesus alone is immortal and living in an unapproachable brightness that no human being has seen or will be able to see. He declares that honor and everlasting dominion belong to God. This spontaneous prayer of praise ends with the acclamation "Amen." It is almost a parallel to the prayer found earlier in this letter (see 1 Timothy 1:17).

The author urges Timothy to warn the wealthy of the world not to be proud and not to set their hopes on the uncertainty of their wealth. Instead, they should learn to trust God who provides us with everything needed for our happiness. The author urges Timothy to tell the rich to perform good works, showing themselves to be generous and ready to share. In doing this, the wealthy will build a true foundation for the future, and not one based on the weak foundation of their possessions alone. Through their generosity, they will receive true, eternal life with God.

Instead of ending his letter in the usual manner used in ending Pauline letters, the author ends with an expression of concern for Timothy. He sums up what he has been saying throughout the letter, namely, Timothy should take care of the gifts entrusted to him and he should avoid all false teachings. He warns Timothy against taking part in worldly babbling and the silliness of so-called knowledge. Some people, by professing this knowledge, have strayed from the faith. The letter ends abruptly, wishing that grace will be with all.

Lectio Divina

Spend 8 to 10 minutes in silent contemplation of the following passage:

The author recognizes the self-deception contained in the arguments of those who speak with assurance about messages they do not really understand. In every age, there are people who have made outlandish statements about creation, denying the existence of God. In some cases, they convey their message as though it were being discovered for the first time, when they are actually reciting attitudes from the past which have been rejected by most people familiar with the scriptures.

Christians strive to discover the truth through reading the revealed word of God in the Scriptures. There is an old saying, "The truth will make you free." Like Timothy, Christians who accept the truth of the scriptures live a life of spiritual freedom in the loving presence of Christ.

✠ *What can I learn from this passage?*

Review Questions

1. What do the author's rules concerning widows reveal about the culture in which the author lived?
2. When the author writes about the rules for presbyters, what does it reveal about the author's attitude toward Timothy?
3. Why did the author accept slavery so easily?
4. What does the author say about those who teach doctrines different from those given to Timothy?
5. In what way can you apply the virtues demanded of Timothy to Church leaders today?

Pastoral Concerns and Christian Behavior

2 TIMOTHY 1—4

If we have died with him we shall also live with him; if we persevere we shall also reign with him. But if we deny him he will deny us. If we are unfaithful he remains faithful, for he cannot deny himself (2:11–13).

Opening Prayer (SEE PAGE 18)

Context

Part 1: 2 Timothy 1—2 The author begins with the usual greeting and thanksgiving. In Paul's name, he offers himself as a model for Timothy to follow, reminding Timothy he has received the true faith. He urges Timothy to remain faithful to the message he has received and to recognize that suffering will accompany those who preach the message of Christ. In preaching Christ's message, Timothy will receive the strength that comes from God. The author, speaking as Paul, points out how everyone abandoned him in the province of Asia, but that one person named Onesiphorus found him and supported him.

Part 2: 2 Timothy 3—4 The author of Second Timothy gives an example of the vices of false teachers and urges Timothy to remain faithful to what he has learned. Recognizing the difficulties Timothy will endure, the author exhorts him to bear hardship like a soldier of Jesus Christ. He must preach Christ's message at all times, when convenient and inconvenient. The author notes Paul's example of faithfully serving the Lord and offers his ministry as a model for Timothy. He urges him to keep his thoughts centered on Jesus Christ. Without mentioning the word "baptism," the author poetically hints that Christians who die with Christ through baptism will live with him, while Christ will deny those who deny him.

PART 1: GROUP STUDY (2 TIMOTHY 1—2)

Read aloud 2 Timothy 1—2.

1:1–5 Greeting and Thanksgiving

As he did in his First Letter to Timothy, the author identifies himself as Paul and sends the letter to "Timothy, my dear child." He again stresses his authority as an apostle of Christ Jesus by the will of God, which means he was chosen by God after Jesus Christ had already ascended. He is called to proclaim the promise of life which is in Christ Jesus. This life in Jesus consists in following the directives of the Gospel message, as well as sharing in the gifts of Christ. The call to live in union with Christ Jesus is a dominant theme of this letter.

The author, continuing to speak as Paul, considered Timothy to be a beloved companion on his missionary journeys and a beloved child, since he views himself as a spiritual father to Timothy. In this letter, the author speaks less formally than in the First Letter to Timothy. He shows his concern not only for the people to whom Timothy ministers, but also for Timothy himself. His intent is to guide Timothy in living a true and faithful life as a disciple of Christ.

The author follows the greeting with a typical thanksgiving prayer. He tells Timothy that he thanks God whenever he thinks of him, which is always. He trusts the faith he has received and can preach it with a clear conscience.

The personal love between Paul and Timothy is expressed when the author describes Paul's sad parting from Timothy and his yearning to see him again. He recalls the sincere faith of Timothy, and the manner in which he received this faith. Just as Paul received his faith from his ancestors, so Timothy has received his faith from his family. The author views the faith of Timothy as having its source in Lois, who is identified as Timothy's grandmother, and Eunice, his mother. The only other reference we have to Timothy's family is in Acts, in which Timothy's mother, although unnamed, is identified as a Jewish woman who was a believer, and Timothy's father is identified as Greek (16:1).

1:6–18 The Gifts Timothy Received

The author notes that Timothy's background is not enough; he must now fan into a flame the faith he received when Paul laid hands on him. In 1 Timothy 4:14, we read that the elders laid hands on Timothy, but here we find out that it was Paul who did so. Perhaps the author chose to add this information here to show that Timothy's authority comes from Paul who truly sent him. Paul himself received his authority and commission by the will of God.

The author adds Timothy did not receive a cowardly spirit, but one of power, tempered by love and self-discipline. In this passage, we see the importance of the apostolic succession. Paul has received the message from the Lord and his ancestors, and Timothy then receives it from his family and from Paul. He is now to pass the Gospel message on to others.

Continuing to speak as Paul, the author urges Timothy never to be ashamed of witnessing to the Lord or be ashamed of Paul for being a prisoner. Paul's image of himself as a prisoner of the Lord takes on a double meaning. He is a prisoner not only in a physical sense due to his confinement in prison, but also in a spiritual sense, as a slave of the Gospel. Timothy must realize suffering accompanies the call to be a disciple of Christ. Christ and Paul have both been treated shamefully, and Timothy must not be ashamed to admit he believes in Christ and supports the message taught by Paul. Like those who went before him, Timothy must be ready to bear sufferings when he preaches the Gospel message, but he will nevertheless have the strength that comes from God to help him through this suffering.

The author writes that Timothy and others share in salvation and holiness, not as a result of any good deeds, but as a gift from God. In God's plan of creation, this gift of salvation and holiness was prepared before the world began and given to the world. The preexistence of this gift makes it all the more significant and emphasizes our inability to merit it. The gift was revealed with the coming of Christ into the world. This appearance of Christ does not refer to the Second Coming of Christ at the end of time, but to the appearance of Christ in his birth, life, and message, and the understanding of this message. Through Christ, death (the power of evil) has been destroyed, and new life and immortality are more clearly seen through the proclamation of the Gospel.

Paul was a herald of this message, an apostle and teacher of the Gospel. He is willingly undergoing hardships for the Gospel, acting without shame and fully trusting Christ will guard the message he has received until the end of time. The author of Second Timothy speaks of the message Paul preached with faith and love of Christ, and he offers it to Timothy as a model to be followed. With the help of the Holy Spirit, who dwells in us, Timothy is to guard this rich deposit of faith. The message, because it is a spiritual one, must have the power of God as its protector. The Holy Spirit, "living in us," provides this power.

Continuing to speak as Paul, the author tells of those who turned against him—namely, Phygelus, Hermogenes, and others who came from the province of Asia. Because the names mentioned here are not found elsewhere, we know nothing more about these people or the manner by which they turned away from Paul. The author may have been speaking of some events in Asia, or an experience he had encountered in Rome between himself and the Asians.

Contrasted with the desertion of those people is the dedication and comfort offered by a person named Onesiphorus. The author prays to the

Lord for the family of Onesiphorus, implying he may already have died. This disciple of Paul refused to be ashamed of Paul's imprisonment. When Onesiphorus arrived in Rome, he immediately searched for Paul and found him in prison. The author prays that Onesiphorus will find mercy with the Lord on the Day of Judgment. He further states Timothy knows better than others the service offered by Onesiphorus at Ephesus.

2:1–13 Timothy's Conduct

The author exhorts Timothy to accept the strength that comes from the grace of Christ Jesus, i.e., the strength that comes from living a life faithful to Christ. He urges Timothy to spread the message he has received from Paul. In this passage, the author is again emphasizing the apostolic tradition of passing on the Gospel message and the practice of the faith. Timothy must teach this tradition to others. Then those who receive it from him must pass it on to others.

Using analogies of a soldier, an athlete, and a farmer, the author urges Timothy to remain dedicated to his call. Like a good soldier of Christ Jesus, Timothy must be ready to accept hardship for the faith. Just as a soldier does not allow himself to become concerned with civilian life, but instead remains faithful to the one who calls him to service, so Timothy should not allow himself to become concerned with the needs of the world, but should instead remain faithful to Christ.

Like an athlete, Timothy cannot win the prize without contending according to the rules. Like the hard-working farmer, he has the first claim to the harvest, the prize of his labors. The author asks Timothy to reflect on these words, and he promises that the Lord will help him to understand them more clearly.

In preaching the Gospel, the author recalls that Jesus Christ, a descendant of David, was raised from the dead. Although Paul often writes in his letters of the resurrection of Christ, he rarely makes reference to the Davidic ancestry of Jesus. As a result of preaching the Gospel message, Paul found he had to endure hardship. The author declares, while the messenger might be shackled like a criminal, the word of God cannot be restrained. For the sake of the elect (Christians), Paul was willing to undergo all suffering so they may come to the salvation that exists in Christ Jesus and may share in the eternal glory of God.

The author introduces a hymn that was apparently popular at the time of the writing of this letter. The hymn states that those who die with Christ will live with Christ, and those who hold firm in the faith will reign with him. Living and dying with Christ is an image used by Paul when he speaks of baptism. In the Letter to the Romans, Paul writes, "We were indeed buried with him through baptism into death, so that, just as Christ was raised from the dead by the glory of the Father, we too might live in newness of life" (Romans 6:4).

In the last lines of the hymn, the author writes that Christ will deny those who deny him, but will remain faithful, even if others are unfaithful. A question arises from this last statement: "How can Christ deny those who are unfaithful and remain faithful to them at the same time?" Commentators explain that Christ can disown those who disown him, but he cannot deny his promise to the community. No matter how many people disown him, Christ will always remain faithful to his covenant.

2:14–26 Foolish and Ignorant Debates

The author urges Timothy to continue to remind the people of the Gospel message and to warn them against squabbling over words. Such squabbling was characteristic of the false teachers who lacked a true understanding of the Gospel, and who led their listeners to spiritual ruin. Timothy must ultimately stand before God as one approved by God, a worker who does not need to be ashamed because he has presented the true message.

The author warns Timothy against profane chatter that only leads to impiety and rapidly spreads ruin to others. He notes this was the problem with Hymenaeus and Philetus, two false teachers who were preaching that the resurrection of Christians had already occurred. As the author pointed out in the First Letter to Timothy, the preaching of a general resurrection having already occurred, coupled with fights over words, led false teachers to call for a withdrawal from the material world (see 1 Timothy 4:1–5 and 6:3–4a). This denial of the goodness of God's creation caused some of these false teachers to forbid marriage and the eating of certain foods.

Such teaching contradicts the truth of the Christian calling to live a new life in Christ brought to us by his death and resurrection.

The message of Hymenaeus and Philetus had apparently been causing some problems at the time this letter to Timothy was written. The author reminds Timothy that the Gospel message does not change. God's foundation is firm and bears the message that the Lord knows those who remain faithful. All those who call on the Lord must turn away from evil.

The author realizes there are both good and bad people in the Church. He compares these people to utensils used in a home. Some are made of gold and silver, and others of wood and clay; some are used for special occasions, and others for common purposes. Those who wish to become special utensils, ready to be used by the owner of the house (the Lord), must safeguard themselves against all evil.

The author warns Timothy to turn away from youthful passions and to practice virtues worthy of Christ. He must "pursue righteousness, faith, love, and peace," just as those who call on the Lord "with purity of heart" do (2:22). He must also avoid all foolish and senseless arguments, which lead to further squabbling. The true servant of the Lord must not be argumentative, but must be a person who is kind to everyone, a good teacher, patient, and gentle in correcting opponents. He must be open to the working of God who may bring people to "repentance that leads to knowledge of the truth," that they might escape the traps of the devil (2:25).

Review Questions

1. What does Paul mean when he says he is an apostle of Christ "by the will of God for the promise of life in Christ Jesus?" What does Paul mean when he says he is a prisoner for the sake of the Lord?

2. What does the author mean when he speaks about the gift bestowed on us in Christ Jesus before time began?

3. How does the author apply the images of a soldier, an athlete, and a farmer to Timothy?

4. How do dying and living with Christ affect our daily life?

Closing Prayer (SEE PAGE 18)

Pray the closing prayer now or after *lectio divina*.

Lectio Divina (SEE PAGE 11)

Relax your body and maintain a posture of prayer (back straight, eyes shut, feet flat on the floor). This exercise can take as long as you want, but in the context of this Bible study, ten to twenty minutes should be sufficient.

The meditations that follow are provided only to help group participants use this prayer form, but note that *lectio* is intended to bring one to a place of prayerful contemplation where the Word of God speaks to the hearer from his or her heart. (See page 11 for further instruction.)

Greeting and Thanksgiving (1:1–5)

Before his conversion to Christianity, St. Augustine felt something was missing in his life. He was searching, and his searching led him to accept some heretical teachings until he learned the truth of Christianity, which led him to dedicate his life totally to Christ. His faith in Christ was built on his desire to serve the Lord. Saint Ambrose had a great influence on the development of the faith of St. Augustine.

Paul built on the faith Timothy received from his family. Although Paul brought Timothy to faith in Christ, Timothy was already a deeply spiritual person seeking the Lord. Paul taught Timothy about Christ and helped him to grow as a fervent apostle of Jesus.

Many people in life already have faith which they received from their families, and many have the good fortune of meeting someone who is able to build on this foundation. This manner of passing on the faith moves from generation to generation. There are also many who did not receive faith through their families, but who had the good fortune of encountering someone who was able to draw out of them a deep love for Christ. Although the Lord provides the seeds of grace, the Lord depends on others to nourish that faith and help it to grow.

✠ *What can I learn from this passage?*

The Gifts Timothy Received (1:6–18)

Christianity, like Judaism, is a historical faith, which means it did not just come with a series of laws. It came through the revelation of history, real people who struggled throughout the Old Testament with their need to believe in the one true God, and the real people of the New Testament who traveled with Jesus and listened to his message. Jesus taught his disciples, and they taught Jesus' message to those who came after them.

Learning about Christ is often a gradual struggle. In Mark's Gospel, we read the story of a blind man healed by Jesus. When Jesus first attempted to heal the man, he sees, but not clearly. He declares he sees people like stumps of trees walking around. The second time Jesus attempted to heal him, the man sees clearly. The message Mark wishes to convey is our understanding of Christ and his message comes gradually, just as it did for Jesus' disciples. It is so deep that we learn how to apply it to our lives slowly, as we mature from one age to the next.

Jesus' message was preached and committed to writing. It was preserved from one generation to the next. It is the message we learned from our ancestors, just as Paul learned his lessons from those who went before him, and just as Timothy learned it from Paul. Christianity is a message that has its links with the preaching of Jesus and the early Church. That is the value of Christianity: its link with the ancestors of our faith and our gradual understanding of the depths of our faith.

✠ *What can I learn from this passage?*

Timothy's Conduct (2:1–13)

Some early Christians had to endure frightening forms of martyrdom in the arena in Rome. Hungry animals would be set free in the arena to attack, tear apart, and eat Christians. Because of the example of courage shown by these early Christians, many of those who witnessed these killings in the arena chose to convert to Christianity. These killings eventually ceased when many of the people of Rome rejected this sickening sight of people being mauled by hungry animals.

Paul the Apostle was willing to suffer for Christ, despite what happened to him. He lists his many sufferings, not for the sake of boasting, but for the sake of being an example of dedication for others. Paul aligned his life with that of Jesus Christ, who suffered and died for us. Paul died to the world with Christ and came to life in Christ. In doing this, he became an example to Timothy and to every Christian.

Christians believe those who do not abandon the Lord will not be abandoned by the Lord. Living this belief can be difficult and demanding, and it is one that Paul wishes to instill in every Christian. With our thoughts centered on Christ, we are called to endure many difficulties in life.

✠ *What can I learn from this passage?*

Foolish and Ignorant Debates (2:14–26)

A preacher on television preached against many other denominations who preached about Christ. He ridiculed them for their manner of worship and their beliefs. At times, he would invite a member of another denomination to come on his program, and when the person appeared, he would ambush him or her with a list of false arguments supposedly taught by their faith. One person who appeared on the program refused to become excited. He simply said, "I can see that you have a closed mind and refuse to listen to what I have to say. So, our discussion must end here." The man stood up quietly and walked off the stage. He believed that entering a heated argument about the faith is not the true avenue for sharing ideas.

The author of Second Timothy warns against foolish and ignorant debates, urging Christians to argue kindly while remaining faithful to the Christian message. Arguments about faith that become heated achieve nothing. When discussing religious matters, Christians should remember the purpose of a debate about religious issues is not to declare who is the winner, but to inform. The author reminds us that teaching about one's faith happens more readily when a person is gentle, able to teach, and tolerant. The author's advice is helpful in our world these many centuries later.

✠ *What can I learn from this passage?*

PART 2: INDIVIDUAL STUDY (2 TIMOTHY 3—4)

Day 1: The Dangers of the Last Days (3:1—9)

The author warns there will be frightening times in the last days. At the time the author wrote this letter, there was a tradition that viewed the devil as making his final futile attempts at turning people against God during the final days of creation. According to that tradition, the sins of the last days will be many, and the author uses a common list to name these sins. Although some of these same sins were found among the people to whom Timothy was sent, not all the people were guilty of these sins.

The author teaches: "People will be self-centered and lovers of money, proud, haughty, abusive, disobedient to their parents..." (3:2). They will be filled with the common sins of the world such as pride, greed, arrogance, abusive language, and a number of ways of acting that destroy humanity. The author warns that although the people served by Timothy act with a show of religious virtue, they are actually denying its power over them. He orders Timothy to reject them, describing how they slip into homes and prey on weak women who are obsessed with their sinful ways and vulnerable to many desires. These women are continually learning something, but they are unable to learn the truth, since the truth is not being taught to them.

In an ancient legend, two magicians, Jannes and Jambres, attempted to deter Moses from leading the Israelites out of Egypt. When Moses' brother Aaron threw his staff on the ground, it turned into a snake, and Pharaoh's magicians matched Aaron's miracle by throwing down their staffs which, in turn, became snakes. Aaron's staff swallowed the magicians' snakes. The Book of Exodus, where this story is found, does not name the magicians, but their names can be found in later Jewish, Christian, and pagan writings (see Exodus 7:8–13).

Like these two magicians, those who teach false truths and erroneous faith are corrupt. Just as people were able to see the foolishness of the two magicians, so will they be able to see the foolishness of those who teach false ideas. Like the magicians, the stupidity of the false teachers will soon be rejected.

Lectio Divina

Spend 8 to 10 minutes in silent contemplation of the following passage:

Many evangelists seem to enjoy speaking of the end of the world and predict that the signs of the end are all around us. They list the evils of the world, the wars and earthquakes, and have no doubt that we are living in the last days. These dire warnings of the end times have been with us for centuries, but here we are, still alive and living in a world of wars and earthquakes that happen over and over again. The last days will happen when God decides. In the meantime, we should live prepared, for our last day will certainly come sometime in our foreseeable future.

Whenever the Scripture writers speak of the last days, they often stress the frightening occurrences which will take place, but many of these dire predictions fall upon those who are sinful. Some predictions of the end of time are presented as a time for those faithful to the Lord to rejoice. What will happen at the end of time remains a mystery, but those who are living close to the Lord will find joy in the coming of the Lord. It will be a time when they realize they are about to spend an eternity with the Lord. The message for all of us is the constant message of the Scriptures, which tells us to be prepared because we do not know the day or the hour.

✠ *What can I learn from this passage?*

Day 2: Paul's Example and Teaching (3:10–17)

Continuing to speak as Paul, the author reminds Timothy to follow his example. Timothy knows what Paul taught about his manner of life: his "faith, patience, love, endurance" (3:10). He is aware of Paul's suffering for the sake of the Gospel at Antioch, Iconium, and Lystra, and he knows how God saved Paul in each of these incidents (see Acts 13:14—14:20). The author tells Timothy that anyone who wishes to preach the Gospel of Jesus Christ must expect to be persecuted.

Those who are evil, who deceivingly look as if they are seeking after the truth, will go from bad to worse. Not only will they mislead others, but they will also be deceiving themselves. Timothy, however, must remain faithful because he knows who his teachers are and what they have taught. The author is referring to those already mentioned in this letter, namely, the family of Timothy as well as Paul himself. Timothy not only learned from these others, but he also learned from the message of the Scriptures.

When the author speaks of the sacred writings, he is not referring to the Christian (New Testament) Scriptures, but to the Hebrew (Old Testament) Scriptures. However, since the author wrote after Paul's death, some commentators suspect that he could also be including Paul's letters in his understanding of the sacred Scriptures. These writings teach wisdom and lead to salvation through faith in Christ Jesus. The author tells us that the Scriptures are inspired by God, and they can be used for teaching, refuting error, correcting, and training in righteousness. Not only do the Scriptures tell us about God; they also serve as a source for training one to live in union with Christ. The Scriptures equip those who belong to God in performing their good works.

Lectio Divina

Spend 8 to 10 minutes in silent contemplation of the following passage:

In the Old Testament, Elisha seeks to gain some of the spirit of Elijah. He does this not only by following Elijah, but by learning from his teachings. When Elijah is finally taken into the heavens in a fiery chariot, Elisha receives his mantle as a sign that the mission and spirit of Elijah have been passed on to him (see 2 Kings 2:1–22). Passing on the message is important in the Scriptures. Jesus passed on his message to his disciples, and Paul passed on his message to Timothy. Timothy had the advantage of learning from one of the most totally dedicated followers of Christ. Paul urges Timothy to follow his (Paul's) example and warns Timothy he will be persecuted for his faith in Christ.

There are martyrs for Christ in the world today, people who are being killed every day for their faith in Christ. Persecution does not necessarily mean being killed for the faith, but facing ridicule, rejection, loss of financial support, or the fear of death. Many times it may be difficult for Christians to live for the Lord as Elijah, Elisha, Jesus, Jesus' disciples, Paul, and Timothy had to do.

✠ *What can I learn from this passage?*

Day 3: Persistence in Preaching (4)

The author tells Timothy to preach the Word of God, whether or not it is convenient or inconvenient. To emphasize his point, the author calls upon Timothy to preach his message before God and Christ Jesus, which implies Timothy should be conscious of the divine presence when preaching. When the author mentions the name of Christ Jesus in this passage, he is speaking of a kingly Christ who will come at the end of time to judge the living and the dead. He also intends to include the total presence of Christ, from the moment he entered our human family until the final judgment day. In his preaching about Christ, Timothy must convince, rebuke, and encourage with the utmost patience in teaching.

The author warns that a time will come when people will not be open to sound teaching but, instead, will seek novel doctrines. Although this time had most likely already occurred before the letter was written, the author makes it appear as though he is speaking of the future. At that time, people would choose teachers to suit their own desires and follow after myths. The author urges Timothy to remain faithful to sound doctrine, enduring suffering, and dedicating himself to preaching the Gospel.

The author, continuing to speak as Paul who was deceased when the letter was written, presents us with a last testimony. He speaks of the end of his life, stating that he is about to depart. He compares his life to the practice used in Jewish worship of pouring out an offering (blood) on an altar to honor God. Speaking of his end with calmness and satisfaction, he states that his life is like a libation being poured out. He has fought the good fight, finished the race, and held firm to the faith. He now looks for the crown that will be given to him on the last day as a result of his dedication. Because he has faith in the Lord as a just judge, he knows he will receive this reward. To avoid a misunderstanding of his message, the author states such a reward awaits all who have longed for the appearance of the Lord with such dedication. Since it is not Paul who wrote these words, the author is using the occasion to praise Paul for his dedication to the Lord right down to the last moment of his life.

This passage continues with a section considered by some commentators to be interspersed with fragments from a letter written by Paul. In this section, the author has Paul speak of his loneliness and his desire to have Timothy join him. Demas, a coworker of Paul, has abandoned him for worldly pursuits. Although we do not know what lured Demas away from Paul, we know from this segment that he left Paul and went to Thessalonica. Other companions also left Paul, most likely to continue their missionary activities. Crescens has gone to Galatia and Titus to Dalmatia. Luke remains with him. The author pictures Paul as telling Timothy to bring Mark with him, saying Mark can be of service, although he does not specifically mention the nature of this service. The author states Paul sent Tychicus to Ephesus.

Adding to the apparent authenticity of Paul as the author of the letter, Paul asks Timothy to bring with him a cloak he left in Troas with someone named Carpus, and to bring his scrolls, especially some apparently significant parchments. This section seems to contradict the author's earlier statement that he will soon be facing death. Here, Paul is preparing for winter, while in the previous section of this passage the author viewed him as preparing for death. Some commentators reason that this is a sign that the second half of this passage concerning preparation for winter comes from a fragment of one of Paul's letters, while the first part concerning his end comes from the pen of the anonymous author.

The author of Second Timothy reminds Timothy of the harm caused to Paul by Alexander the coppersmith, and he assures Timothy the Lord will repay him for what he has done. Meanwhile, he warns Timothy that he must also beware of Alexander, since the coppersmith has resisted not only Paul but also the message Paul preached, the same message preached by Timothy.

Paul repeats his message of loneliness which he felt when he was put on trial for his preaching. No one supported his testimony and all abandoned him. He apparently accepts their weakness at such a time and does not wish this lack of support to be held against them. The Lord, however, did help him, and he received such strength that it enabled him to complete the preaching ministry to which he was called and to carry the message to all nations.

Paul speaks of bringing his message to the ends of the earth. During Paul's era, many people viewed a trip to Rome as symbolically a trip to the ends of the earth. Through his ministry in Rome, Paul would symbolically be bringing the message to all nations. With the Lord's help, he was saved from the "lion's mouth," that is, from those who wished to kill him.

Because of the help received from the Lord in the past, Paul can declare with confidence his faith that the Lord will keep him from all harm and will bring him safely to the heavenly kingdom. This thought leads to a spontaneous prayer of praise for the Lord.

The passage ends with the usual practice of sending greetings to those who are with Timothy, namely, Prisca, Aquila, and the family of Onesiphorus. Paul informs Timothy that other companions such as Erastus and Trophimus remained in other cities, the first at Corinth, and the second, because of an illness, at Miletus. His loneliness again becomes apparent when he urges Timothy to attempt to arrive before winter. He sends greetings from the Christians in the place where he is staying, especially from Eubulus, Pudens, Linus, and Claudia. He ends with the customary liturgical greeting, praying Timothy will share in the grace that comes with the Lord's presence.

Lectio Divina

Spend 8 to 10 minutes in silent contemplation of the following passage:

Although we are aware of Jesus' agony in the garden and the cruelty he endured when he was scourged and nailed to the cross, an agony often overlooked is the agony of being abandoned by his friends at the moment of his death. Many relatives of dying patients sit with them throughout the night, not wanting them to die alone. Our desire to be present with the loved one at the time of that person's death touches the lives of many of us. We often overlook the sadness and loneliness Jesus must have felt when only his mother, a few women, and the beloved disciple were with him when he was dying.

The Second Letter to Timothy offers another insight into the personality of Paul. He is dedicated, ready to offer his life for Christ, but he also shows how truly human he was when he expresses his feelings of loneliness. Like the loneliness of Jesus at the time of his death, the loneliness Paul experienced is a suffering many overlook. When we read his letters, he can sound so firm and strong, yet he admits he, like many others, can suffer from loneliness. In every way, his life offers an example of what it means to love Christ.

✠ *What can I learn from this passage?*

Review Questions

1. What does the author mean when he says there will be terrifying times in the last days?
2. Why does the author believe that all who live religiously in Christ Jesus will be persecuted?
3. What does the author say about the use of Scripture?
4. Why does the author tell Timothy to preach the Gospel message whether or not it is convenient or inconvenient?
5. What does Paul mean when he says he is being poured out like a libation?
6. If Paul is so conscious of the Lord's presence, why does he experience loneliness?

Living Christian Life

TITUS 1–3

For the grace of God has appeared, saving all and training us to reject godless ways and worldly desires and to live temperately, justly, and devoutly in this age, as we await the blessed hope, the appearance of the glory of the great God and of our savior Jesus Christ (2:11–13).

Opening Prayer (SEE PAGE 18)

Context

Part 1: Titus 1—2 The author, speaking as Paul, identifies himself as a slave of God and apostle of Jesus Christ, serving for the sake of the faith of God's chosen ones. He declares that he left Titus at Crete that he might establish right order and appoint presbyters. He lists the conditions necessary for presbyters and bishops and exhorts Titus to teach sound doctrine to older men and women, to younger men, and to slaves.

Part 2: Titus 3 The author suggests ways of living in peace with the government. He also warns Titus to avoid all useless and philosophical arguments or ideas proposed by Jewish converts who wish to impose Jewish customs on all converts to Christianity. He admits he was once foolish and disobedient, but the generous love of God helped him. He received God's gift of salvation, not as a result of any good work, but because of God's mercy. This came to him through his baptism and the gift of the Spirit. He ends by instructing Titus to encourage his listeners to devote themselves to good works.

PART 1: GROUP STUDY (TITUS 1—2)

Read aloud Titus 1—2.

1 Pastoral Concerns

The letter begins by identifying Paul as the sender, but most commentators believe it is written by an unknown author who used Paul's name, believing he is faithful to Paul's teachings. The author, speaking as Paul, states he is a servant of God and an apostle of Jesus Christ who was sent to lead the chosen ones to a greater knowledge of faith and truth. Paul was totally dedicated to his mission of sharing faith in Christ with all people.

The author states Paul performed his mission, hoping in the eternal life promised "before time began" by God, who never lies (1:2). In using this phrase, he is saying this was God's plan from all eternity. Christians seek the truth with the hope of attaining everlasting life with God. At the proper time, God revealed the mystery of salvation and entrusted its proclamation to Paul.

Continuing to speak as Paul, the author addresses the letter to Titus, whom he calls his "true child in our common faith" (1:4). Since Paul converted Titus to the faith as he did with Timothy, he believes he has a right to call him his child. The greeting ends with a wish for grace and peace "from God the Father and Christ Jesus our Savior" (1:4).

The author says that Paul left Titus in Crete in order to finish what was left undone and also to appoint presbyters in every town. As part of Paul's evangelization of an area, he would train leaders to act as elders or presbyters in his absence. The presbyter must be without fault, married only once, with children who are not unruly or rebellious, but true believers (1:6). He then applies his message to bishops. When the author speaks of bishops in this passage, he is apparently putting them on a par with the presbyters and is not speaking of the office of bishop as we understand it today.

The qualifications for presbyters and bishops are similar to those found in the First Letter to Timothy. The bishop, as God's steward, must be blameless. He must not be arrogant, quick-tempered, a heavy drinker, violent, or greedy. In contrast, he must be hospitable, a lover of goodness, sensible, just, devout, and self-controlled. In a period when false teachings were being spread among the people, the author states a bishop must be a man who faithfully follows sound doctrine and is capable of presenting the true faith and refuting those who argue against it.

The author warns Titus there are many people in Crete who teach empty and false messages, especially among the Jewish converts to Christianity. Such people should be silenced. They are hurting entire families with false teachings, and they are doing this not for any religious reasons, but for the sake of monetary gain. The author quotes an ancient statement from a prophet in Crete accusing the Cretans of being liars, evil animals, and lazy gluttons. Looking at those who have accepted false teachings, the author apparently agrees with this ancient judgment of the people of Crete.

The author instructs Titus to correct the people with harshness, not for the sake of hurting them, but for the sake of keeping them faithful to sound doctrine and away from the Jewish myths and rules invented by those who have rejected the truth. One of the teachings of Jewish converts to Christianity was that certain foods were unclean, but the author reminds Titus that all things are clean for those who are clean (faithful to the true teachings of Christ), and that all things are corrupt for those who are corrupt themselves. Their corruption reaches into their mind and conscience. Although they claim to have knowledge of God, their actions prove otherwise. The author ends with harsh words for these false teachers. He calls them detestable, disobedient, and totally incapable of any good actions.

2 Christian Behavior

The author instructs Titus to preach a message that contains sound doctrine. The first group Titus should address are the older men, who must be "temperate, dignified, self-controlled, sound in faith, love, and endurance" (2:2). He must then address older women, telling them that they must act in a manner fitting for those who belong to God. They must be reverent in demeanor, not spreading slander, not addicted to drink, and teaching what is good. By their manner of acting, they must train the younger women to love their husbands and their children. The example of the older women should also lead younger women to be self-controlled, chaste, good household managers, kind, and submissive to their husbands. Because of their good actions, the Word of God will not be discredited.

The author urges Titus to instruct the younger men to be self-controlled. He informs Titus that he should be an example by performing good works, and his teaching should reflect integrity, seriousness, and sound speech that cannot be ridiculed. Such behavior has practical results for Christians living in the world. Opponents will be put to shame by their inability to speak evil of the community. Since the author has already expressed his belief that the Cretans are liars and lazy gluttons, he believes the good example of Christians can have an effect on their manner of acting.

The author then addresses slavery. During the era in which Titus lived, slavery was an accepted practice. At this point in history, Christianity showed no concern about changing the social structure. The masters wanted obedient, not rebellious, slaves. To keep peace in the accepted social order of the day, the author urges slaves to be submissive to their masters, to please them, and not to contradict them or steal from them. They should be faithful to their masters so others will give credit to the teaching about God, whom the author calls "our Savior." This term "Savior" is often used for Jesus, but rarely in relation to God.

The author informs Titus the grace of God has appeared, meaning it is known through the preaching of apostles such as Paul. This grace offers salvation to all people, not just to the Jews. Through this sound doctrine, Christians are trained in virtue, rejecting godless ways of acting and all worldly ambition. Christians are trained to live with personal discipline, with justice and devotion in this age, and to live with a hope for the coming manifestation of the glory of "our great God and of our savior Jesus Christ" (2:13). Jesus Christ is the one who sacrificed himself for us, to free us from every power of evil, and to purify us so we could belong fully to him with a desire to perform good deeds.

The author exhorts Titus to preach this message, instructing and correcting with full authority. He directs Titus not to allow anyone to look down on him.

Review Questions

1. What does the author mean when he speaks of Paul as dedicating himself to preaching to the people "in the hope of eternal life" (1:2)?
2. Why does the author, speaking as Paul, address Titus as his true child?
3. What does the author think of the people of Crete?
4. What virtues does Paul require for those chosen to be spiritual leaders of the people?
5. Why is it important for Titus to give good example to the younger men?
6. Why does the author say nothing about the evils of slavery?

Closing Prayer (SEE PAGE 18)

Pray the closing prayer now or after *lectio divina*.

Lectio Divina (SEE PAGE 11)

Relax your body and maintain a posture of prayer (back straight, eyes shut, feet flat on the floor). This exercise can take as long as you want, but in the context of this Bible study, ten to twenty minutes should be sufficient.

The meditations that follow are provided only to help group participants use this prayer form, but note that *lectio* is intended to bring one to a place of prayerful contemplation where the Word of God speaks to the hearer from his or her heart. (See page 11 for further instruction.)

Pastoral Concerns (1)

A woman, who had a great devotion to St. Francis de Sales, told an audience she often tried to follow the example of St. Francis, who began each day meditating on the presence of God in his life. Before she left her bed, she would say to herself ten times, "God is with me! God is with me!" Then she would roll out of bed with the thought God was present with her in every action of her day.

During his life on earth, Jesus taught his disciples the Beatitudes, which consisted of a list of spiritual attitudes expected of his followers. In one of the Beatitudes, Jesus states: "Blessed are the clean of heart, for they will see God" (Matthew 5:8). The author of the Letter to Titus states: "To the clean all things are clean" (1:15). To be clean of heart means to see God in every joy and difficulty of life. This is God's creation.

In the Beatitudes and the Letter to Titus, those who live with an attitude of remaining faithful have developed an attitude of seeing God in creation. The woman who could say "God is with me" saw God in creation. As the Beatitude states, "Blessed are the clean of heart, for they will see God."

✠ *What can I learn from this passage?*

Christian Behavior (2)

An atheist, a political prisoner in a concentration camp, became Christian because he saw another prisoner, a Christian, share his meager meals with others who were ill. After the war ended and the prisoners were freed, the atheist went to a pastor in his area and said he wanted to become Christian, because he met Christ in the concentration camp.

Central to the message the author shares with Titus is the need for good example. When we dedicate ourselves to Christ, others become aware of our religious beliefs and expect us to live up to them. Christians teach about their faith not only by speaking about Christ, but by living an exemplary life. Many people have become Christian because they saw the good deeds of those who profess faith in Christ.

✠ *What can I learn from this passage?*

PART 2: INDIVIDUAL STUDY (TITUS 3)

Day 1: The Goodness of God (3:1–8a)

The author tells Titus to remind Christians about their civic duties regarding obedience to officials of the government and those who represent them. The importance of living in peace with the social structure of the day continues to hold a high place in the letters of the early Christians. The Letter to Titus continues to stress the idea of good works and good example. Christians must perform their work honestly, avoid all slander and quarreling, and be courteous with all people.

The author reminds Titus that all unbelievers lacked virtues in the past and were foolish, disobedient, led astray, and living as slaves to their passions and pleasures. He includes himself among those who lived without faith. Their ignorance and lack of virtue caused havoc for them and for the social structure. They lived in wickedness and envy, were despicable, and hated one another. All this changed, however, when the kindness and love of God appeared and saved them, not because of any good deed they performed, but because of God's generous love and compassion.

The author alludes to this salvation as coming through the new birth in the waters which he calls the "bath of rebirth" (3:5). This is a reference to baptism, a rebirth brought about by the Holy Spirit. This gift, he explains, comes to us through Jesus Christ, our Savior. The author continues to use the title Savior for Jesus and God. This gift of baptism was given so that Christians might be justified by Christ's grace. They receive the call to live as heirs, looking forward with hope to eternal life. As in the Letters to Timothy (1 Tim 1:15; 3:1; 4:9; 2 Tim 2:11), the author guarantees the correctness of his teaching with the formula, "This saying is trustworthy" (8a).

Lectio Divina

Spend 8 to 10 minutes in silent contemplation of the following passage:

> Jesus tells the story of a man whose servants work all day in his
> field. When they come in at night, he does not tell them to sit down
> at the table so he can wait on them, but he expects them to prepare

a meal for him. Jesus tells us that even when we have performed good works, we are still servants of the Lord.

Jesus is the master and we are the servants. Our salvation depends totally on the goodness and mercy of God. If we lived a perfect, sinless life, God would still not owe us eternal joy. Jesus, however, promised that those who remain faithful will share in eternal life. We can expect that those who live a life of loving God and one's neighbor will receive an eternal reward. The reward does not come because God owes it to us, but because a loving God desires to share it with us. The reward for those who remain faithful to the Lord is always a gift from God.

✠ *What can I learn from this passage?*

Day 2: Advice to Titus (3:8b–15)

The author urges Titus to stress his message about the Gospel so that those dedicated to God will continue to perform good works. These virtues and works are excellent and helpful to all. During the era in which Titus lived, many teachers were posing false and superstitious arguments and genealogies. Since these were common false teachings confronting Christianity, the author tells Titus he must refrain from arguing about the law. The author is most likely warning Titus to avoid arguments with the Judaizers. The Judaizers were Christian converts from Judaism who wish to impose Jewish laws and customs upon the new converts from among the Gentiles. Apparently familiar with the futility of these discussions, the author knows such arguments are pointless.

The author then directs Titus to follow the custom of warning a heretic once and, if needed, a second time. After that, he should have no more to do with the heretic, since he has already fallen into sin and condemned himself. The author is telling Titus that the person, because he is not open to listening to any warnings, has chosen to condemn himself.

In the final farewell, the author provides a glimpse of the missionary activity of the early Church. Artemas and Tychicus are mentioned as possible replacements or companions to Titus. Since the author asks Titus to join him at Nicopolis where he intends to spend the winter, Titus' work at Crete seems to be coming to an end. The author directs Titus to send Zenas, a lawyer, and Apollos on their journey. Commentators speculate that Zenas could be either a Jewish scribe or a man versed in Greek and Roman law. Apollos is apparently the Alexandrian Christian mentioned in the Acts of the Apostles (Acts 18:24—19:1). The sending community has the responsibility of supporting the missionaries. The author directs Titus and the people of Crete to provide these missionaries with everything they need for their journey.

The author urges the people to perform worthwhile work in order to care for their needs. He states that all his companions send greetings and directs them to pass these greetings onto "those who love us in the faith" (3:15), i.e., to all Christians in Crete. He ends by praying that God's grace will be with all of them.

Lectio Divina

Spend 8 to 10 minutes in silent contemplation of the following passage:

A man with severe arthritis worked in a soup kitchen feeding the poor people of the neighborhood with a warm meal for lunch and dinner. Those who ran the soup kitchen had difficulty getting volunteers, and they were happy for this man to be working with them. People would watch him as he hobbled from table to table serving the meals. Whenever someone asked him why he endured such excruciating pain to serve those in need, he would reply that someone had to do it, and he was happy to help others.

The author of Second Timothy believes that the followers of Christ should devote themselves to good works because good works are beneficial to others. When Christians live as Christ commanded, others benefit, since Christianity is based on the need to work for the common good. Besides love of God, Christians are called to love of neighbor. Many people benefited from the good works of Paul the Apostle, who dedicated his life to good works. He is an example of Christian living which was beneficial to others. The man with arthritis is not only helping others, but he stands out as an example of a man who believes in his call to help others, no matter how difficult the cost. Christians have the call to help others without counting the cost.

✠ *What can I learn from this passage?*

Review Questions

1. How, according to the author, does the Lord train us to reject godless ways and worldly desires?
2. What makes the author say he was once foolish?
3. Does the Lord save us because of our righteous deeds?
4. What is the bath of rebirth and how does it affect our life?
5. How do the good works of Christians benefit others?

Jesus, Compassionate High Priest

HEBREWS 1–6

In times past, God spoke in partial and various ways to our ancestors through the prophets; in these last days, he spoke to us through a son, whom he made heir of all things and through whom he created the universe (1:1–2).

Opening Prayer (SEE PAGE 18)

Context

Part 1: Hebrews 1—2 In the Old Testament, God spoke to us through the prophets, and in the current era, God speaks to us through the Son, who is far superior to the angels. God created the earth and the heavens which will perish, but the Son, who is eternal, will never perish. God attested to the magnificence of the Son, who was made for a period a little lower than the angels when he lived among us in his human form to free all people from slavery to sin. He had to become like us, his brothers and sisters, in every manner except sin in order to become a faithful and merciful high priest before God.

Part 2: Hebrews 3—6 Although Moses was worthy of God's blessings, the Son is still superior to Moses. Just as Moses was faithful among the Israelites, Christ was faithful as a Son placed over all people. Those who remain faithful belong to the house of Christ. Christians are warned to avoid evil and not live with a heart that is unfaithful to God. Those who wandered in the desert with Moses were unfaithful, and God promised they would not enter into God's rest, i.e., into the Promised Land. Christians must remain faithful or they will not enter into the eternal rest of the Lord, which is heaven. Jesus who gave his life for us is a compassionate high priest who took upon himself our human condition and who, like other high priests, is taken from among humanity for this eternal office. The followers of Jesus must move beyond the basic teachings of the law and move on to a mature knowledge of Christ. Jesus became a high priest according to the order of Melchizedek, which is a reference to an existence as an eternal high priest.

PART 1: GROUP STUDY (HEBREWS 1—2)

Read aloud Hebrews 1—2.

1:1–4 Sharing the Word of God

The opening lines of this letter introduce its theme—the importance of Christianity in contrast to Judaism. In the past, God spoke to our ancestors through the prophets in a limited and diverse manner, but now, in the last days, God speaks to us through the Word of God who is the Son dwelling among us. The author does not deny the importance of God's Word as given to the Israelites, but he proclaims that the last days have arrived when the Word of God comes to us with the highest authority, namely the life, death, and exaltation of the Son.

When the author of Hebrews speaks of the last days, he does not mean the world will end soon, but the times in which all people are now living are the last days. These are the days when the promises made to Abraham, Moses, and the prophets have reached their fulfillment. We are living in the era of the "last days."

In ancient cultures, sons often had a right to their father's inheritance.

The author speaks of God as having appointed the Son as an heir. In using this reference of appointing the Son as an heir, the author is speaking of Jesus, who became one with us and brought us to a new inheritance with him. He is the Son, the Messiah who inherited all of creation. Besides being appointed to inherit all, the Son is the one through whom the world was created.

The author informs the reader that the Son reflects the glory of God and is the very image of God's nature, thereby implying that the Son is one with the Father. In ancient times, a stamp was impressed in wax to prove a message or gift came from a particular person. In speaking of the Son as the very image of God's nature, the stamp or copy of God's nature likewise shows the Son is a living presence of God in the world. God made the universe and keeps it in existence, and the Son shares in this same mission.

The author continues with a major theme of the letter by telling us the Son cleansed us from our sins and has taken his place at the right hand of the Majesty (God) on high. The right hand is the place of honor and power. The one closest to a king sat at his right hand. Sitting at the right hand of God, "the Majesty from on high," refers to the exaltation of the Son that took place through the death, resurrection, and ascension of Jesus Christ, by which he attains our purification from sins.

A significant message is the Son is superior to the angels. Angels played a major role in ancient writings. The rabbis and other Jewish leaders viewed them as intermediaries of God. These religious leaders believed God was far too exalted to enter directly into human affairs, so angels acted as God's messengers, bringing the law of God to the people. Such power and responsibility naturally placed the angels in a high position, and the author of Hebrews now informs us the Son holds a more exalted position than the angels. This position is as far above the angels as the title he bears, namely, the title of Son.

The author continues with a major theme of the letter by telling us the Son cleansed us from our sins and has taken his place "at the right hand of the Majesty on high" (1:3). The right hand is the place of honor and power. The one closest to a king sat at his right hand. Sitting on the right hand of God, the Son, Jesus Christ, is exalted through his death, resurrection, and ascension, which attains our salvation.

A significant message is that the Son is superior to the angels. Angels played a major role in ancient writings. The rabbis and other Jewish leaders viewed them as intermediaries of God. These religious leaders believed God was far too exalted to enter directly into human affairs, so angels acted as God's messengers, bringing the law of God to the people. Such power and responsibility naturally placed the angels in a high position, and the author of Hebrews now informs us the Son holds a more exalted position than the angels. This position is as far above the angels as the title he bears, namely, the title of Son.

1:5–14 Messianic Enthronement

Using a series of seven Old Testament quotations, the author continues to show the Son is far more exalted than the angels. Five of these quotations speak of the special position held by the Son in relation to the Father, and two of them refer to the angels and their role as servants who worship the Son. Many commentators allude to the messages of the following quotations as enthronement psalms, identifying the place of the Son before the Father.

The author quotes first from Psalm 2:7, an enthronement psalm used for the kings of ancient Israel: "You are my son; this day I have begotten you" (1:5a). In its application by the author of Hebrews, the psalm tells us that God calls Jesus "my son." The psalm has its origin in the ancient attitude toward adoption which taught that the son belonged to the adopting father to such a degree the father could claim to have given birth to the son. The unity of God and the Son is the major theme of this passage.

Although Christians believe the Son was always God, the author of Hebrews is revealing the relationship between God and the Son. When the author applies Psalm 2:7 to the Son, he is stating the Son is truly begotten of God, exalted above the kings and even above the angels. The writer asks if God had ever applied these words to any of the angels. The unspoken answer is "no." The second quotation is from 2 Samuel 7:14, where God, through the prophet Nathan, enters a covenant with David, making him the ancestor of a royal "house." The Lord said, "I will be a father to him, and he shall be a son to me" (1:5b). This quote in its original context defines the relationship between God and the Davidic ruler as that of father to son. The author applies this Scripture text to Jesus and has God state that God will be a Father to Jesus and Jesus will be a Son to the Father.

The third quotation is taken from the Greek translation of the Old Testament (Deuteronomy 32:43) and is not found in the Hebrew text. The quote reads: "Let all the angels of God worship him" (1:6). In its original context, the author invites all the angels to praise God, while the author of Hebrews uses it as an invitation to the angels to worship the Son, revealing his superiority over the angels.

The fourth quotation comes from Psalm 104:4: "He makes his angels winds and his ministers a fiery flame" (1:7). The author adapts this song of praise to God and applies it to the ministry of the angels who were messengers and ministers of God. Although the original text did not intend to establish a lower position than the Son to the angels, it is used in contrast to the quotations that follow, which will speak of the higher position held by the Son.

The fifth quotation is taken from Psalm 45:6–7, a second enthronement psalm which speaks of the throne of God standing forever, a throne of righteousness and justice, one that hates wickedness. The author applies this psalm, which was also originally applied to God, to the Son, an expansion of the message concerning the Son of God given in verses 2 and 3 of this letter. New kings were anointed with oil, usually a joyful occasion. The author applies the psalm to the Son, who is anointed with the oil of gladness. The psalm speaks of the unending reign and power of the Son, who has served righteousness and justice faithfully and who has received the place of honor above all kings.

The sixth quotation comes from Psalm 102:25–27, and it speaks of the Lord as establishing the earth and heavens which will perish, but the Lord will remain for years without end. The Son (Lord) will live eternally, but creation will end, rolled up like a cloak and changed like a garment. The Son will live eternally the same, without change.

The seventh and last quotation comes from Psalm 110:1, the third royal psalm used in this series. It speaks of the Son taking the exalted position of honor and power at the right hand of God. This exalted position will place the Son so far above those who reject him that they will be seen as his footstool.

Now that the author has spoken about the Son's exalted position over the angels and his relationship to the Father, he asks a question (really a statement) about the lower position of the angels. He asks whether or not they have the role of ministering spirits with the duty of serving those who are to obtain salvation, namely human beings. The implied answer is "yes."

2 Exhortation to Faithfulness

Throughout the letter, the author not only gives an explanation of the Scriptures in relation to Jesus Christ, but also adds periodic exhortations, calling his listeners to respond to his message. At the beginning of this second chapter, the author reminds his listeners they should pay special attention to the message of Jesus, the Son.

The author urges his audience to listen attentively to the message of Jesus so they are not carried away. When the author speaks of being "carried away," he is apparently referring to those who ignore Jesus' message. He reminds his listeners that the angels brought a message which was unchangeable and which brought punishment for those who transgressed or disobeyed it. If the word brought by the angels could not be ignored without punishment, how could anyone hope to ignore the promised salvation without facing punishment? This promised salvation comes from Jesus.

The author realizes his audience is two or three generations removed from Jesus, and he recalls for them that this Word of God was first given by Jesus and passed on to them by those who listened to him. Those, who passed on this message, received from God the power to perform signs, wonder-filled deeds, and miracles. Through God's will, they also received the gifts of the Holy Spirit. These signs were meant not to exalt them, but to point beyond them to the message they preached.

Looking forward in time to the world that is to come, the author of Hebrews tells his audience God did not make the future world subject to the angels. He develops his message by quoting from Psalm 8:4–6, inter-preting the text to fit his message. The original text speaks of the high position held by human beings in God's creation. God is ever mindful of them, placing them a little lower than the angels, crowning them with glory and honor, and making all things subject to them. In the story of the creation of Adam and Eve, God made all of creation subject to them.

The author applies this text about all things being subject to them to Jesus rather than human beings. Jesus shares our nature which is a little lower than the angels. In subjecting all things to Jesus, there was noth-ing which was not subject to him. Although we do not yet see all things which are subject to Jesus, we believe Jesus is "crowned with glory and honor" (2:9), because he died for us. By the grace of God, Jesus, the Son, experienced death for everyone.

Since God had the aim of bringing all people to glory, it was fitting the one to lead people to salvation should be made perfect through human suffering. In becoming flesh, the Son becomes more like us. The author speaks of the people as "many children," thus showing a relationship of all people with Christ. Because the one who sanctifies and the ones who are sanctified have the same origin, who is the God the Father, Jesus the Son is able to call them brothers and sisters. The author quotes from Psalm 22:23, in which the psalmist declares he (the psalmist) will proclaim the Lord's name to his brothers and sisters and "in the midst of the assembly" (2:12). The author of Hebrews also applies this Scripture text to Jesus, who will proclaim the name of God to his brothers and sisters.

The author then quotes from Isaiah 8:17–18, in which Isaiah declares he will put his trust in the Lord. The author of the letter makes Jesus the speaker who proclaims he will put his trust in God, and he is present with the children given to him by God. Because of his sharing fully in human nature, Jesus, by his death, was able to snatch away the devil's power over death. This freed all who were slaves living in fear of spiritual death, because they now had an opportunity for salvation through Jesus.

The author of Hebrews notes the Son did not come for the sake of the angels, but to help the descendants of Abraham. The author is speaking of all human beings as children of Abraham. To atone for the sins of all and to become a compassionate and faithful high priest before God for all human beings, it was necessary for the Son to take upon himself our humanness. He had to become human. Because he himself was tested as they were, he is able to help others who are being tested.

Review Questions

1. List some characteristics of the Son as presented in the first chapter of the Letter to the Hebrews.
2. How can Jesus be considered a little lower than the angels?
3. Why did Jesus have to become like us?
4. What does the author mean when he says he had to become like his brothers (and sisters) in every way?

Closing Prayer (SEE PAGE 18)

Pray the closing prayer now or after *lectio divina*.

Lectio Divina (SEE PAGE 11)

Relax your body and maintain a posture of prayer (back straight, eyes shut, feet flat on the floor). This exercise can take as long as you want, but in the context of this Bible study, ten to twenty minutes should be sufficient.

The meditations that follow are provided only to help group participants use this prayer form, but note that *lectio* is intended to bring one to a place of prayerful contemplation where the Word of God speaks to the hearer from his or her heart. (See page 11 for further instruction.)

Sharing the Word of God (1:1–4)

With every gift comes responsibility. Living after Jesus Christ came into the world and revealed that he was the Son of God is a privilege shared by Christians. It is not, however, something we merited, but a gift of history which comes to us through the mysterious plan of God. We have the privilege of knowing that Jesus is the Son of God who became human and dwelt among us, and we also have the responsibility of accepting Jesus' message as the true Word of God.

In the story of the Wedding Feast of Cana in John's Gospel, Jesus changes water into wine. When he does, the headwaiter tasted the wine and said to the bridegroom, "Everyone serves good wine first, and then when people have drunk freely, an inferior one; but you have kept the good wine until now" (John 2:10). The symbolism here compares the Old Testament with the New. The better wine begins when the Word became flesh. The Letter to the Hebrews tells us, "in these last days, he spoke to us through a son," referring to the arrival of Jesus in the world. The author praises Jesus as being higher than the angels.

The reading reminds us as Christians we have the privilege of knowing Jesus as the Christ and the Son of God, and the responsibility of responding to that privileged message.

✠ *What can I learn from this passage?*

Messianic Enthronement (1:5–14)

At the end of the Church year, Catholics celebrate the feast of Christ the King. In many church buildings throughout the world, the assembly will hear the same message. The throne for Jesus Christ the King is not a majestic, golden throne, but a cross. Christ is king because Christ became one with us, suffered, and died, and was exalted as the savior of the world. Christ is our king, not just to be worshiped, but to be imitated. By becoming human like us, Christ not only preached his message, but Christ also gave us an example of how to live his message. In the Letter to the Hebrews, the author tells us about the exaltation of Jesus Christ which is based on his willingness to join our human family.

Jesus Christ, the exalted one, is one with God and higher than all the angelic hosts of heaven. When we read the Old Testament, we recognize the hidden message that God planned from all eternity to have the Son come into the world. Jesus said, "Do not think that I have come to abolish the law or the prophets. I have come not to abolish, but to fulfill" (Matthew 5:17). Jesus' life and exalted position is the fulfillment of the Old Testament law and the prophets. The people of Old Testament times never envisioned a messiah who would be a divine person and who would bring us salvation by joining our human family. The present concept of Christ the King is far different from the concept of God as king in the Old Testament. Christ has given us a new understanding of God's great love for us.

✠ *What can I learn from this passage?*

Exhortation to Faithfulness (2)

Jesus became one with us to bring us salvation. The author shows how fitting it is that a loving God should experience our human condition. In the Acts of the Apostles, Luke writes, "There is no salvation through anyone else, nor is there any other name under heaven given to the human race by which we are to be saved" (4:12). That God would become human to bring us salvation was far beyond anyone's imagining, yet we can ask, "What God is like our God?" The people who worshiped false gods worshiped gods who were selfish, jealous, cruel, and conniving. The author of Hebrews is telling us Jesus, who is God, joined our human family, called us brothers and sisters, and saved us. The challenge for Christians is to live as brothers and sisters of Jesus Christ and of each other.

✠ *What can I learn from this passage?*

PART 2: INDIVIDUAL STUDY (HEBREWS 3—6)

Day 1: Entering the Rest of the Lord (3—4:13)

The author begins by inviting his listeners to reflect on Jesus, who is an apostle (one who is sent by God) and high priest, who brings us salvation, and offers praise to God. Jesus was faithful to the Lord who sent him, in the same way as Moses was faithful to his call in serving the Lord. The author tells us that Jesus is "worthy of more 'glory' than Moses," just as the builder of a house is more honored than the house itself (3:3). Every house has a builder, and God, as creator, is the builder of all things.

Moses was a faithful servant in God's household, witnessing to mysteries that would later be revealed. Christ, however, as the faithful Son, became master of the house and, as master, is worthy of all praise. We belong to the house of Christ and must confidently remain firm in hope.

The author quotes from Psalm 95:7b–11, which speaks of the journey of the people of Israel through the desert under Moses, who hardened their hearts against the Lord. The people rebelled against God, who became angry and swore they would never enter into his rest. In the Exodus story, the rest they sought during the Exodus was entry into the Promised Land. The rest in the Letter to the Hebrews refers to resting in God.

In using Psalm 95, the author of Hebrews makes some changes for the sake of his message. The author warns his listeners against allowing an evil and faithless spirit to lead them away from the living God. He urges them to encourage one another daily while they are living in the present moment ("today"), so their hearts do not become hardened by the deceitfulness of sin. Having been given a solid foundation, they will remain heirs with Christ only as long as they remain faithful to that foundation.

The author of Hebrews again quotes from Psalm 95:7b–8a, which warned the people of Israel not to harden their hearts like the people of the Exodus who had revolted. The author asks his listeners to pay attention to those with whom God was angry, stating they were the ones who came out of Egypt with Moses. Because of their disobedience, the sinful generation of Israelites did not enter into the Lord's rest. It was their lack of faithfulness that prevented them from entering God's rest.

The author warns that those who hear the word of God in this letter could, like the Israelites of the Exodus, choose to ignore God's voice and rebel against the Lord by becoming disobedient and unfaithful. Like those who revolted in the desert, the word of the Lord would be of no profit to them, and they would not enter God's rest.

In speaking of God's rest in these passages, the author includes several ideas of rest, such as resting in the Promised Land, celebrating on the seventh day a day of rest, which is the Sabbath, and resting in the peace of God's Presence. God promised the people of Israel they would enter the land of rest—the Promised Land. The author applies this promise in a spiritual sense to resting in God's presence, to which all people are called. Just as the people of Israel lost their chance of entering the Promised Land, disobedient Christians could lose their chance of entering the spiritual Promised Land.

Christians received the Good News as the people of Israel had, but the Israelites did not respond to the message with faith, so it did them no good. Christians, however, who respond in faith, share in that promised rest. The author once again quotes from Psalm 95:1–11, stating that God swore in anger that the Israelites would not enter into the Lord's rest.

The author of Hebrews alludes to God's act of creation and the fact that God rested from his work on the seventh day (Genesis 2:2). Although God, through the words of the psalmist, said some would not enter into God's rest, there are some who will enter it. The promise of God is as much present today as it was during the Exodus. In Psalm 95, the psalmist warns the people not to harden their hearts when God calls them "today," meaning every new day. The Sabbath rest and resting in God's presence is seen as the same by the author of Hebrews. Upon entering the Promised Land, Joshua provided a day of rest for the people. The Sabbath rest existed from the time of creation, and it was meant to be a time of rest in God's presence.

The author ultimately ties the rest of the Promised Land together with the Sabbath rest to show the promise continues. The people are called to a rest marked by the serenity of entering into the very presence of God. The author exhorts his listeners to be faithful to the Gospel message in order to attain this rest and avoid the disobedient and unbelieving example of the Israelites in the desert.

The author of Hebrews introduces a hymn concerning the power of the living Word of God. At the beginning of the letter, he spoke of the power of God's Word coming through the prophets and living in the Son. He now tells us the Word is alive and active, and it cuts even more finely than a two-edged sword. This living Word cuts deeply into every life. This is shown when the author speaks of severing the joints from the marrow, which is considered the material part of life. Using this image, he applies it to severing the soul from the spirit, which is the spiritual part of life. The Word cuts so deeply that it can judge the thoughts and intentions of one's heart.

The author tells us this Word of God lays bare all of creation. We must always keep in mind the Word of God is the living action of God. Nothing can be hidden from God, to whom we must give an accounting of our lives. The Word of God is creative and sees all that we do.

Lectio Divina

Spend 8 to 10 minutes in silent contemplation of the following passage:

A man, whom God blessed with a loving wife and three healthy sons, prayed often and never missed worshiping each Sunday with his family. After fifty-three years of marriage, his wife died and he became angry with God. He turned against God, refusing to pray and to participate in Sunday worship. If God were going to treat him this way, then he would harden himself against such a God. One day, his eldest son angrily confronted him, telling him that he only loved God when God was good to him. He stated this was not love of God, but love of self. The elderly man listened to his son, realizing he never thanked God for the blessings of fifty-three years with his wife, and he turned humbly back to God and Sunday worship. His heart again rested in the Lord.

Once Christ promised salvation to the world through his life, death, and exaltation, Christians have a greater hope of resting in the Lord for all eternity. The warning is we must not harden our hearts against the Lord, but must remain faithful. Salvation is not automatic. If we wish to rest in the Lord for all eternity, we must rest in the Lord during our life, i.e., we must remain faithful to the law of love given by Christ, no matter what happens to us. Jesus is "'Emmanuel,' which means 'God is with us'" (Matthew 1:23). God is always present with us, and we rest in the Lord when we live with an awareness of this gift. We must love the Lord in good times and in bad.

✠ *What can I learn from this passage?*

Day 2: Jesus, Compassionate High Priest (4:14—5:10)

In an earlier passage (2:17), the author spoke of Christ as the merciful and faithful high priest. He has already shown us the faithfulness of Christ as the Word of God, and he now speaks of Christ as the compassionate high priest. In the Old Testament, the high priest passed through the veil (or curtain) of the Temple into the Holy of Holies. The author of Hebrews

---

refers to this image when he pictures Christ, the high priest, as passing through to the highest heaven. Since we have such a high priest, we should hold firm to the hope we have received from Christ.

Christ is not a distant high priest who misunderstands us, but one who can sympathize with us because he became one with our human condition. Although he was tempted as we are, Christ never succumbed to sin. Because of Christ, the high priest, we dare to approach the throne of his graciousness with confidence in order to receive mercy, grace, and help in our times of need. The author reveals that we have in Christ a compassionate high priest who has proved his love for us by becoming one with us. This fills us with hope and confidence.

The author of Hebrews refreshes the listener's memory about the necessary requisites for becoming a high priest in Israel. The high priest is not angelic, but a human person, taken from among human beings to serve as their representative before God. His duty is to offer gifts and sacrifices to God on behalf of the people. His presence in the human family means he also shares in the weaknesses and sinfulness of human nature, and he offers these gifts and sacrifices to God on his own behalf as well as on behalf of others. No one chooses the office of high priest, but it comes as a call from God to the chosen offspring of Aaron.

The author elucidates how Christ fulfills these requisites, beginning with the last one mentioned and working his way toward the first. Christ did not take on himself this office of high priest, but received it from God. The author quotes from Psalm 2:7b, which pictures God as telling Jesus, he is God's chosen Son, begotten "today." He also quotes from Psalm 110:4b, which pictures God as telling Jesus Christ he is a priest forever according to the order of a priest named Melchizedek. Melchizedek was a priest who offered a sacrifice for Abraham in the Old Testament. In this passage, Christ is called a priest (not a high priest) according to Melchizedek. (More information about Melchizedek will be found in Hebrews 7:1–10.)

Since the high priest is one taken from among human beings, the author alludes to Jesus during his earthly life. Jesus offered prayers and supplications with loud cries and tears to God, the one who could save him from death. Although some commentators point to specific events in Jesus' life when he called out to God for help (such as the agony in the garden), most commentators believe more emphasis should be placed on the idea Jesus prayed in a human fashion rather than at a specific moment in his life. Jesus shared in our human suffering and offered prayer to God. Human weakness is one of the requirements for becoming a high priest. Jesus fulfilled this requirement.

Because of his obedience, Christ's prayer was heard. The idea of obedience in the New Testament not only refers to acts of obedience; it also refers to a harmony of one's will with that of God. Jesus was always faithful to God's will. "[H]e learned obedience from what he suffered" (5:8). When he was perfected through his passion, death, and exaltation, Jesus brought salvation to all who obediently served him. Being in harmony with the Son's will was the same as being in harmony with the Father's will. Because Christ fulfilled these requirements so well, God designated him high priest according to the order of Melchizedek.

Lectio Divina

Spend 8 to 10 minutes in silent contemplation of the following passage:

A pastor told the story of a woman whom he believed was a mystic. He said she loved to pray and sing with the assembly during their Sunday liturgy, and she declared she felt ecstatic as she ended each prayer "through Christ our Lord. Amen." She believed Christ changed her life so she was no longer worshiping in her name alone, but in the name of Jesus. She learned Jesus gave his life that she might participate in and not just attend liturgy as a spectator. In liturgy, she learned a truth that touched her deeply, namely, that she was in union with Christ worshiping God the Father.

Christ became human to become our eternal high priest. He suffered like all human beings and, instead of offering the blood of animals, he offered his own life. Through baptism, Christians share in the priesthood of the faithful that is a share in the priesthood of Jesus Christ. Christians worship in the name of Christ. The ordained priest, to a different degree, also shares in the priesthood of Jesus Christ.

Through our priesthood, given to us by Jesus, we worship God the Father in Christ's name. This is a privilege which comes to us from Christ the high priest.

✠ *What can I learn from this passage?*

Day 3: Jesus' Eternal Priesthood and Sacrifice (5:11—6:20)

The author interrupts his line of thought with an exhortation concerning the inability of his listeners to learn mature teachings. They have become dull in understanding. Instead of being able to teach others, they need someone to teach them the basic principles for understanding God's message. Like infants, they need milk and not solid food. In his letters, Paul speaks of the most basic teachings as milk, and he declares some people are ready for solid food, while others, young in the faith, are only ready for milk. The author's implication in this letter is the people should have been far beyond the milk stage by now.

Those living on the milk of basic teachings are not yet ready to receive the more mature teachings of the Church. Solid food (solid doctrine) is for those who are "mature, for those whose faculties are trained by practice to discern good and evil" (5:14). The author urges his listeners to move from the basic teachings about Christ and to more mature teachings. The author identifies a list of basic teachings: "repentance from dead works and faith in God, instruction about baptisms and laying on of hands, resurrection of the dead and eternal judgment" (6:1–2).

The author has harsh words for believers who have fallen away. These believers include those who have been brought to the light, tasted the gifts from heaven, shared in the Holy Spirit, and tasted the goodness of God's message and "the powers of the age to come" (6:5). If they fall away, it becomes impossible for them to be renewed. This message caused problems for some members in the Early Church. Some believed the letter proved there was absolutely no hope for those converts who fell back into their sinful ways. The author views these sinners as people who are crucifying Christ all over again and holding him up to ridicule. Christian teaching today recognizes that sinners do have hope for forgiveness if they repent.

The author turns to an Old Testament image of a field and its harvest. He speaks of a field that drinks in the rain created by God and "brings forth crops," or good fruit (6:7). Such a field, like a person who produces good works, receives a blessing from God. In contrast, a field that brings forth briars and thorns is worthless. The crop is cursed, and in the end burned. Here the author's analogy refers to those who have received God's Word but have not used it correctly, thus making themselves worthless and destined to be burned.

Now that the author has warned his listeners about their weaknesses and the impending dangers of apostasy (turning against the God in whom they once believed), he turns his attention to their goodness. Despite all he has said thus far, the author of Hebrews assures his listeners he believes they possess a better side that points toward their salvation. He declares that God does not ignore their deeds and the love they show in serving "the holy ones" (6:10). This phrase, though often used interchangeably with "saints" in Scripture, refers to believers in the past and the present rather than a select group of canonized men and women. The author encourages them to bring his hopes to fulfillment by not becoming sluggish, but instead living as imitators of the faithful who shall inherit God's promises.

The author states that God swore to bless Abraham and to multiply his offspring. Abraham waited patiently for the fulfillment of the Lord's promise. The author views the promise made to Abraham as being fulfilled in Christianity. The Lord's sworn oath to Abraham is true, since there is no one greater than the Lord. Since an oath is meant to end all arguments, human beings swear by someone greater than themselves. When God wanted to confirm a promise, God intervened with an oath. God cannot lie.

The author continues to dwell on the idea of taking an oath, i.e., affirming that people swear by someone greater than themselves. A promise is strong and acceptable, and an oath gives it more strength. Since no one would deny a promise accompanied by an oath, God used an oath to prove more firmly to the heirs of the promise that the Lord's intention would not change. God's oath does not depend on another, since there is no one greater than God. God's promise would have been enough, but God chose two means, a promise and an oath, to show God's plan would be fulfilled.

This provided the heirs with the firm hope that the fulfillment of God's promise would be fulfilled.

As a link with the message that is to follow, the author tells us Jesus entered beyond the curtain before us and for our sake. The imagery of the curtain brings us back to the temple image of the Holy of Holies, which no one could enter except the high priest. Jesus Christ is our "high priest forever according to the order of Melchizedek" (6:20).

Lectio Divina

Spend 8 to 10 minutes in silent contemplation of the following passage:

Someone once said Catholics can confess their sins to the ordained priest on Saturday and commit the same sin on Tuesday. This statement is a misunderstanding of the sacrament of reconciliation. The person who confesses sins must have the intention of not committing that sin again. The person, through human weakness, may commit the sin again, but at the time of confessing it, the person must have a sincere intention of avoiding this sin in the future, or the sin is not forgiven.

Christians have learned to trust the forgiving love of the Lord. The Lord is willing to forgive over and over again. When people repent, the Lord looks into the person's heart. Jesus said, "Not everyone who says to me, 'Lord, Lord,' will enter the kingdom of heaven, but only the one who does the will of my Father in heaven" (Matthew 7:21). Just calling on the Lord or seeking forgiveness with no intention of changing one's life does not bring forgiveness. The Lord looks into our heart, not only to the words we utter.

✠ *What can I learn from this passage?*

Review Questions

1. How is Jesus superior to Moses?

2. What is important about the Sabbath rest as found in the Letter to the Hebrews?

3. Why is it necessary for Jesus to be a compassionate high priest?

4. Who were the high priests in the Old Testament?

5. Why was it necessary for Jesus to become human in order to attain the role of eternal high priest?

6. What does the author say about those who were converted to the Word of God and later rejected it?

7. How does taking an oath affect the promise made by God?

Jesus, A Priest Forever

HEBREWS 7–13

It was fitting that we should have such a high priest: holy, innocent, undefiled, separated from sinners, higher than the heavens (7:26).

Opening Prayer (SEE PAGE 18)

Context

Part 1: Hebrews 7—8 Melchizedek was the priest who blessed Abraham, which made him superior to all the descendants of Abraham. Since the story of Melchizedek ends abruptly with no word about his parentage or death, the author considers him to be a symbol of the eternal priesthood. Christ is this eternal priest according to the order of Melchizedek. Christ's priesthood is not merely an earthly priesthood, but a heavenly priesthood. With Christ, the new high priest, the old law ceases and a new law begins.

Part 2: Hebrews 9—13 The author contrasts the priests of the Old Testament with the priest of the New Testament, namely Jesus Christ. The priests of the Old Testament had to be obedient to the covenant of Moses, but Christ as the new and eternal high priest brought a New Covenant. In the Old Testament, the high priests entered a tabernacle (room) made by human hands, but Christ passed through a tabernacle not made by human hands. In the

Old Testament era, there were many high priests who succeeded each other, and there was a need to offer many sacrifices. In the New Testament era, there is one high priest and the one sacrifice of Jesus Christ. Christians share in the life of this new high priest of the New Covenant.

Even though the leaders of the ancient family of Israel lived by faith, they never saw the fulfillment of the promise made to them by God. This fulfillment is Jesus Christ. Christians should endure their trials as a form of discipline to make them faithful followers of Christ. Those who are disobedient will receive a punishment. In the end, Christians should live with a mutual love for one another.

PART 1: GROUP STUDY (HEBREWS 7—8)

Read aloud Hebrews 7—8.

7 Melchizedek, the Eternal Priest

In this chapter, the author reveals further the meaning of the eternal priesthood of Jesus Christ. As a model for the eternal priesthood of Christ, he refers to the Old Testament story of Melchizedek, a priest who blessed Abraham. The Book of Genesis speaks of Melchizedek, the king of Salem, who brings bread and wine to Abraham. The author of the Genesis story informs us Melchizedek was a priest of God Most High. Melchizedek blessed Abraham, and Abraham acknowledged the power of Melchizedek's blessing by offering a tenth of everything he had to him (see Genesis 14:18–20). Melchizedek's story ends here; nothing more is said about his coming and going.

The author of Hebrews applies Melchizedek's priesthood to the priesthood of Christ. In Hebrews, we learn the name Melchizedek means "king of righteousness," and the phrase King of Salem means "king of peace." Since the Book of Genesis provides no parental background or ancestry for Melchizedek and makes no mention of the beginning or end of his life, the author of Hebrews pictures him as eternal, declaring Melchizedek is a priest forever, like the Son of God.

In ancient times, the people believed offspring were contained in the loins of their ancestors, which meant all of Abraham's offspring were considered to be in his loins. The descendants of a person, i.e., those in his loins, were considered to be less than those who went before them. Following this belief, the author of Hebrews explains the greater position of Melchizedek over the priests of Israel. Melchizedek was greater than Abraham because he blessed Abraham who accepted the blessing. Since he was greater than Abraham, he is therefore greater than Abraham's offspring.

The priests of the Old Testament came from the tribe of Levi, who was one of the twelve sons of Jacob and a great-grandson of Abraham. Since Levi came from the loins of Abraham, he and the priests were not considered to be as great as Abraham. The people of Israel paid a tenth of their wealth to the priests from the family of Levi, just as Abraham had given a tenth of his wealth to Melchizedek. Because of this offering given by Abraham to Melchizedek, Levi, Abraham's descendant, is also seen as having made an offering to Melchizedek through Abraham, thus making Melchizedek the greater priest.

The author now explains why Christ is considered a priest according to the order of Melchizedek. In the Old Testament, the Lord directed Moses to ordain as priests Aaron and his sons, descendants of Levi (see Leviticus 8—9). If the Mosaic Law had established the perfect priesthood, why would there be a need to provide another priesthood according to the order of Melchizedek? The implication is that the priesthood of the Mosaic Law was not a perfect priesthood.

Since the descendants of Levi were priests under the law, then a change of priesthood would bring about a change of law. The new priesthood would not come under the Mosaic Law. With Christ as the new high priest, the Law of Moses would cease, so a new law would come into existence. Jesus was a descendant of the tribe of Judah, and Moses said nothing about priests of the tribe of Judah. The offspring of Judah were not priests and never ministered at the altar.

The author of Hebrews states that it becomes more obvious if someone is made a priest in a different way, according to the order of Melchizedek. In this case, we are not speaking of someone chosen according to the Mosaic

Law, who receives it because he belongs to a specific tribe, but one chosen by the power of an indestructible life that comes from the power of God. The author pictures God applying the words of Psalm 110:4 to Christ: "The Lord has sworn and will not waver: 'You are a priest forever in the manner of Melchizedek" (see 7:17).

This order of priesthood according to Melchizedek offers the pledge of a better covenant than the Old Covenant with Moses. Since the old law could not offer perfection, the new priest annuls the former covenant. Because each priest under the Law of Moses died, they had to be replaced. Unlike the many priests of the Old Covenant who died, Jesus, since he remains forever, has a priesthood that never ends. By fulfilling his priestly role forever, he is always able to offer salvation to those who approach God through him.

The author of Hebrews declares, "It was fitting that we should have such a high priest: holy, innocent, undefiled, separated from sinners, higher than the heavens." (7:26). In offering himself, Jesus the high priest made the perfect sacrifice once and for all, a sacrifice that needed no repetition as did the sacrifices offered by the high priests of old. The law, in its imperfection, chose men prone to weakness as high priests. But the Word of God, who swore an oath after the old law ceased, chose the Son, who has been made high priest forever.

8 The New Covenant

In the previous passage, the author stated that Christ's priesthood is greater than that which existed according to the law and which involved men only during their lives. The author continues to speak about other ways in which the priesthood of Christ is superior to that of the Levitical priesthood.

The author first tells us the priesthood of Christ is far superior because it does not involve a merely human office in life, but a far higher position, namely, the exalted position "at the right hand of the throne of the Majesty in heaven" (8:1). Our new high priest is the minister of the sanctuary and the true tabernacle established by the Lord. In the Old Testament (Exodus 25:1–9), we read about the meeting tent established by God for the Israelites.

This tabernacle of old is contrasted with the new tabernacle established by the Lord (see about the Tabernacle in the Introduction, page 19).

The author tells us that every high priest has the duty of offering gifts and sacrifices, and Christ, as high priest, must also have something to offer. When Jesus was on earth, he was not a priest under the Law of Moses, since the offering prescribed by the law had already chosen priests from the family of Levi to make the offering. The sanctuary used by the priests of the law was only a copy of the heavenly one. The author quotes from Exodus 25:40, in which Moses is given directives to make the tabernacle according to the pattern given to him on the mountain. He believes Moses saw the heavenly sanctuary and was only able to make a vague copy of it. Such a view is in line with the author's belief that the physical world is only a poor copy of the reality of the spiritual world. Because Jesus lives in the real, spiritual world, he has received a far higher ministry than that of the priests of the law. He is a mediator of a superior covenant, founded on promises more exalted than those of the Old Covenant.

The author indicates the need for a second covenant by exposing the imperfection of the first. The imperfection lies with the covenant itself and with the Israelites' response to it. The author quotes from Jeremiah 31:31–34, which speaks of a New Covenant to be made with Israel in the days to come. In the first covenant, God led the people from Egypt and gave them the law, but the people broke the covenant. The New Covenant, however, will be different; the law will be written in their minds and hearts, all shall know the covenant, and their sins will be forgotten. The author reminds us that the mere idea of a "new" covenant means the older one is obsolete and ready to pass away.

Review Questions

1. Who is Melchizedek and why is he so important in this letter?
2. What contrasts does the author make between the many high priests and sacrifices of the Old Testament and the high priesthood of Jesus Christ?
3. What does the author mean when he speaks of the heavenly priesthood of Jesus Christ?
4. How did the Old Covenant become obsolete?
5. How does the priesthood of Jesus Christ affect us?

Closing Prayer (SEE PAGE 18)

Pray the closing prayer now or after *lectio divina*.

Lectio Divina (SEE PAGE 11)

Relax your body and maintain a posture of prayer (back straight, eyes shut, feet flat on the floor). This exercise can take as long as you want, but in the context of this Bible study, ten to twenty minutes should be sufficient.

The meditations that follow are provided only to help group participants use this prayer form, but note that *lectio* is intended to bring one to a place of prayerful contemplation where the Word of God speaks to the hearer from his or her heart. (See page 11 for further instruction.)

Melchizedek, the Eternal Priest (7)

At the Easter Vigil, the Presider blesses the Easter Candle with the words, "Christ yesterday and today, the beginning and the end, the Alpha and the Omega, to him belongs time and the ages, to him be glory and empire, throughout all the ages of eternity. Amen." Christ is God, and therefore has no beginning and no end. We cannot comprehend this mystery with our limited minds, but with the insight of faith, we can proclaim that we believe it.

It is fitting Jesus Christ be made the eternal priest, since he became flesh and joined our human family and lives eternally. Jesus Christ, however, does not keep this gift to himself. Christians share in the eternal priesthood of Jesus who made the greatest offering anyone could make, namely the sacrifice of his life. This one priesthood, which is a share in the priesthood of Jesus Christ, will continue on earth until the end of time. Jesus is a priest forever according to the line of Melchizedek.

✠ *What can I learn from this passage?*

The New Covenant (8)

The New Covenant demands that people dedicate themselves to Christ the high priest, not by offering animals, but by turning one's mind and heart to the Lord. The New Covenant does not count how much a person offers, but the spirit and dedication of the person making the offering. The greatest offering has already been made by Jesus Christ. At the Last Supper, Jesus took bread and said, "This is my body," and he took a cup of wine and said, "This is my blood of the covenant, which will be shed for many" (see Mark 14:22–24). In the celebration of the Eucharist, Catholics join in the greatest sacrifice ever made, the sacrifice of the body and blood of Jesus Christ. After this, there is no greater sacrifice that could be made. When Catholics celebrate the Eucharist, they join with Jesus, the eternal high priest, in the celebration of his Last Supper.

✠ *What can I learn from this passage?*

PART 2: INDIVIDUAL STUDIES (HEBREWS 9—13)

Day 1: Sacrifice of Jesus (9)

The author speaks of the tabernacle and sacrifice of the Old Covenant. He draws some of his ideas about the tabernacle from Exodus 25 and 26, which speak of the collection and materials used in the construction, and he adds some details not found in Exodus. He claims he is following the laws for worship and for the sanctuary, but some of his descriptions likely originate from an oral tradition and not a written source. The author describes the tabernacle clearly and precisely, telling us the outer part, called the Holy Place, contained the lampstand, the table, and loaves for presentation. This part was used every day by all the priests.

The inner tabernacle, called the Holy of Holies, was entered through a veil by the high priest only once a year, on the Day of Atonement. The author provides us with a clear description of the inner tabernacle, remarking on the golden altar of incense and the Ark of the Covenant, both of which held a place of honor within the Holy of Holies. According to Hebrews, the contents of the ark were "the gold jar containing the manna, the staff of Aaron that had sprouted, and the tablets of the covenant." According to the Old Testament, the manna and the staff of Aaron were placed in the tabernacle, but not in the ark (see Exodus 16:33–34 and Numbers 17:25–26). The tablets of the covenant (the commandments) were placed in the ark. Over the ark were symbols of two glorious cherubim who hovered over the seat of mercy. The offering of the high priest on the Day of Atonement was the offering of blood (animal sacrifice), which he offered for himself as well as for the people.

The author interprets the presence of the outer sanctuary as if it were a hindrance to entrance into the second tabernacle, the Holy of Holies. As long as it exists, he tells us, no one has a right to enter the inner sanctuary. He claims this message comes from the Holy Spirit, and he speaks of this condition as a symbol for the "present time," likely a reference to a previous time when the tabernacle described by the author once existed, rather than the time at which the author is writing. This passage cannot be used as evidence the Temple was still standing. The gifts and sacrifices offered under this condition could never bring worshipers to perfection, since they were concerned only with regulations of the flesh, namely, regulations concerning food, drink, and ritual washings, that were imposed only until it was time to reform them.

The author's message is that as long as the Old Covenant existed, with its specific type of sacrifice and priesthood, the world would be kept back from the Holy of Holies. When Christ came as the high priest of all the blessings that have come, he entered the more perfect tabernacle, which was not made by human hands. This is the heavenly tabernacle Christ entered once and for all. The author is contrasting this entrance of Christ into the heavenly tabernacle with the entrance of the priest into the earthly tabernacle into which he enters once each year.

In the previous passage, the author spoke of the blood sacrifices offered by the high priest. The author notes Christ also made an offering of himself when he entered the heavenly tabernacle. The offering, however, was made "not with the blood of goats and calves but with his own blood, thus obtaining eternal redemption" (9:12).

In the Israelite sacrifice, the blood of goats and bulls and the sprinkling of the ashes of a heifer were utilized for the purification of those who had defiled their flesh in any of the many ways mentioned in the Mosaic Law. The author contemplates how much more effective is the blood of Christ, who offered himself as a perfect sacrifice to God through a spirit which is eternal. This idea of a spirit does not refer to the Holy Spirit, but to the life and spirit of the risen Christ, which is an eternal spirit. His offering cleanses us from our dead and sinful works and allows us to worship the living God.

Christ is the mediator of the New Covenant, canceling by his death the sins committed under the Old Covenant. Those who are called will receive the promised inheritance. The author speaks of a testament, likening it to a type of will. A will, for example, can only be effective if the person who makes it is dead; conversely, a will serves no effective function if the person who makes it is alive. Following this line of thought, the author states even the first covenant needed some death or blood-giving involved in it.

The author expands on Exodus 24:3–8 in describing how Moses, after he had announced the commandments to the people, took the blood of goats and calves and some water and sprinkled the book and the people using scarlet wool and hyssop. While he did this, he proclaimed that he was using the "blood of the covenant" commanded by God. He also sprinkled the blood on the tabernacle and all the vessels used for worship. The author tells us the law requires everything to be purified by blood, since there is no forgiveness without the shedding of blood.

The author continues to speak of the material world as a copy of the spiritual reality. The world had to copy the heavenly models when offering sacrifice, but the heavenly realities called for a better form of sacrifice. The reason for the more perfect sacrifice was that Christ was not entering a sanctuary made by human hands, one which is a mere copy of the true sanctuary. Instead, he was entering the highest sanctuary, heaven itself, to appear face-to-face with God on our behalf.

Unlike the high priest who must enter the Holy of Holies year after year with blood that is not his own, Christ does not have to offer himself over and over again. If this were necessary, then Christ would have to die over and over again from the beginning of creation. Instead, Christ has appeared once for all at the end of the age to do away with all sin by the sacrifice of himself.

Just as human beings are destined to die only once and then to be judged, so Christ offered himself once for all to bear the sins of many. The author makes a rare reference to the Second Coming of Christ. He states Christ will come a second time, not with the purpose of taking away sin, but to bring to salvation those who are eagerly awaiting him.

Lectio Divina

Spend 8 to 10 minutes in silent contemplation of the following passage:

At every celebration of the Eucharist, the memorial of Christ's passion, death, and exaltation is celebrated. The celebration of the Eucharist is not another celebration separate from the Last Supper, but a celebration in union with the Last Supper. It is a living memorial. There is one eucharistic celebration just as there is one high priest who is Jesus Christ. Every time we celebrate the Eucharist, we are celebrating the one supper of the Lord. This is a great mystery given to us through the life, death, and exaltation of Jesus.

When Jesus died on the cross, the veil of the Temple was torn down the middle, symbolically opening the Temple's Holy of Holies to all the people (see Luke 23:44–46). Jesus opened a spiritual Holy of Holies in which all those who celebrate the sacrament of baptism enter with Jesus, the high priest. The Holy of Holies is no longer a place where a priest could enter only once a year. The new Holy of Holies is the presence of the kingdom of God on earth. All are invited to enter this Holy of Holies which Jesus brought to us by his death, resurrection, and ascension. Christians believe there is one high priest, one Lord, one sacrifice, and one celebration of the Eucharist in which Catholics throughout the world celebrate in union with Christ.

✠ *What can I learn from this passage?*

Day 2: One Sacrifice Instead of Many (10)

The author summarizes what has already been stated. Following his philosophical view of creation, the author tells us the law never had the power to bring worshipers to perfection by the same sacrifices offered year after year, since the law, as all material things, is only a shadow and not a true image of the good things to come. If this were not so, then the priests would have stopped offering sacrifices, since the worshipers, once purified, would have no consciousness of sin. Instead, there is a yearly reminder of sin reflected in these sacrifices. The blood of bulls and goats cannot possibly take away sins.

The author then references Psalm 40:6–8, picturing Jesus as speaking to God, stating God prepared a body for him because God did not desire any sacrifice or offering (10:5–6). Jesus has come to do the will of God as it is written in the Scriptures. The author interprets this psalm as a sign God took away the first covenant in order to establish the second. God did not desire the sacrifices and offerings of the Old Covenant, so Jesus came to do God's will. By following the will of God, Jesus brought salvation by offering his body once for all.

The author once again repeats his message that other priests perform their duties daily, offering over and over again the same sacrifices that are not able to remove sins. Jesus, however, has offered one sacrifice for sins and has taken his place at the right hand of God, where he is now waiting until his enemies are placed beneath his feet. By the one single offering of himself, Jesus has brought eternal perfection to those whom he is sanctifying.

All of us, through the blood of Christ, have the right to enter the sanctuary. This belief is in sharp contrast to the Old Covenant, in which only the high priest could enter the sanctuary. This is the new way given by Christ, an opening through the curtain procured by Christ, the great high priest who presides over the house of God. We enter the sanctuary fully purified, with a sincere heart, that is, a heart filled with faith and sprinkled clean of any trace of an evil conscience, and our bodies cleansed with pure water.

Reminding his listeners of the faithfulness of God, the author encourages them to hold firmly to their hope. They, in turn, should encourage one another to love and to perform good deeds. They should not neglect the assembly, as some do, but should urge one another to participate in these meetings (a reference apparently to the celebration of the Eucharist). They should be even more concerned about this as the Day of Judgment draws near.

The author warns those who would turn back to sin that no other sacrifice will save them. They will face the judgment and the fire faced by those who rebel. Fire is a popular image used to portray God's judgment on sinners. In Moses' Law, a person who sins is put to death by the witness of two or three people. The author warns that those who spurn the Son of God and profane the blood of the covenant will receive a far harsher punishment.

Those who rejected the Law of Moses faced death by stoning, and those who deny Christ can expect a far more horrible spiritual death. The author quotes from the Book of Deuteronomy, which speaks of the vengeance and judgment of the Lord (Deuteronomy 32:35–36). Although God is merciful and loving, the author warns it is a frightening thing for sinners to fall into the hands of the living God, i.e., judgment by God.

The author writes about the sufferings of those who accepted faith in Christ. He speaks of their enlightenment, which may be a reference to their entry into the Church through the rite of baptism. Those who accepted the faith are reminded of the days when they were publicly exposed to insults and trials, or when they were associated with those who were treated in this manner. With the knowledge of a better and more lasting reward, these Christians were also willing to join with those who were in prison and to accept being stripped of all of their possessions. The author urges them not to lose confidence, since they will receive a great reward. He tells his listeners that they will need patience to do God's will and gain what God has promised. The author is apparently not speaking of a specific persecution, but is instead referring in general terms to various types of suffering endured by Christians of his own time.

The author quotes from Isaiah (26:20), who states he who is to come will come soon, and he follows this quotation with one from the prophet Habakkuk (2:3–4), who states that the Lord is pleased with the just one who lives by faith, but that he finds no pleasure in one who shrinks back. The author ends this passage by joining himself with his listeners, declaring he and they are not the type who shrink back and perish, but are among those who keep their faith and are saved.

Lectio Divina

Spend 8 to 10 minutes in silent contemplation of the following passage:

> Christians have endured suffering and death in many areas of the world since the time of Jesus. Many of these Christians acted heroically despite the pain and torture they had to endure. For Christians, Jesus is the ultimate example of accepting suffering and remaining faithful to God. The sacrifice for Christians is not an offering of the blood of animals, but an offering of oneself, either by living a Christian life despite rejection and ridicule. Jesus said, "No one has greater love than this, to lay down one's life for one's friends" (John 15:13). Jesus viewed all people as friends. Christians who lay down their lives for Christ or for others are following the example of Christ and showing by example the great love Christ had for all people.

✠ *What can I learn from this passage?*

Day 3: Faith of the Ancients (11)

This chapter begins with a brief definition of faith and then offers examples or models of faith from the creation of the world to the story of the Israelites in the Old Testament. It shows the masterful mind of the writer, who carefully draws his images from significant Old Testament characters and events. Providing a full interpretation of this text would demand going back into the history of all the people mentioned and analyzing the gradual development of their faith and the challenges they faced in living that faith. Consequently, we will touch only on those people and events, rather than delving into the many examples of faith found in their lives.

The opening line provides a definition of faith, the meaning of which in the original Greek is not easily grasped. Most commentators read the definition as stating faith is an assurance or guarantee of things hoped for, and a conviction that things we don't see really exist (11:1). Some commentators, however, interpret the text as a reference to the objects of faith rather than to the person who has this assurance and conviction. These commentators would see faith as the real existence of those things hoped for and the proof of those things not seen. A person would then respond to such faith. In either case, the author is able to state that the people of the past received God's approval for their life of faith.

Although the author will be speaking of the people of the past and their faith, he begins with God and God's creation of the universe and suggests that faith helps us to understand the work of the Word of God. Through faith, we believe God, who is invisible, exists from all eternity, and the Word of God created the world. What is visible was created by the invisible.

The author refers to the story of Cain and Abel (Genesis 4:1–16), in which God was pleased with Abel's offering, but not with Cain's. When Cain killed Abel, God punished him. The author teaches that God was pleased with Abel's sacrifice because it was offered in faith. By accepting Abel's offering, God testifies to the pleasing gift. Even though Abel is dead, the message of his faith continues to speak to us.

Another model for faith is Enoch, who presumably did not die, but was taken up into heaven by God because of his faith (Genesis 5:24). The author concludes that a person must have faith to please God. It is this faith that informs us of God's existence and of the rewards God gives to those who seek God.

When Noah was warned by God about those things that were to happen, he responded with faith and built the ark to save his family. By his faith, he condemned the world and inherited righteousness. The Old Testament writers contrasted the faith of a good person with that of an evil person. When we recognize goodness, we also recognize evil, its opposite. In this way, the faith of Noah stands in contrast to the lack of faith on the part of others who refused to live by faith.

By his faith, Abraham obeyed God. Unaware of where he was going, Abraham journeyed to the country that would be his inheritance and that of his descendants (Genesis 12:1–4). He lived in the Promised Land, a foreigner in a strange country, dwelling in tents as did Isaac and Jacob, the heirs of the promise (Genesis 23:4; 26:3; 35:12). By faith, Abraham believed his wife Sarah would conceive a child, although she was already past the childbearing age. Because he trusted God, Abraham, who was almost dead himself, was able to bring forth descendants whose number would be as numerous as the stars in the sky and the sands on the seashore (Genesis 22:17).

All of these people died in faith, although they had not obtained what was promised. They saw themselves as strangers and foreigners on earth seeking their real homeland. They could not have been thinking of the land from which they came, since they could have easily returned there. Instead, they were longing for their heavenly homeland. Because of their faith, God, who has established a heavenly city for them, does not hesitate to be called their God.

The author continues to speak of the faith of Abraham as evidenced by his willingness to sacrifice his only son Isaac at God's command (Genesis 22:1–8). Abraham's faith was truly tested because he knew God had promised that his descendants would carry on his name through Isaac. He also knew God was able to raise the dead, and God's saving of Isaac from the brink of sacrifice was a symbol of Christ's resurrection.

Through faith, Isaac blessed Jacob and Esau (Genesis 27:1–40), knowing the result of these blessings would continue into the future. Jacob, when he was dying, blessed each of Joseph's sons and worshiped God through his faith in this action (Genesis 47:31—48:22). When he was near death, Joseph also acted with faith when he foresaw the Exodus from Egypt and planned his own burial in the Promised Land (Genesis 50:24–26).

In the story of Moses, we read he was hidden by his mother from those who were killing the male children of the Israelites, and he was saved from death by the Pharaoh's daughter, who found him and raised him in the royal court. When Moses was discovered after killing an Egyptian soldier in an attempt to defend one of his countrymen, he had to flee from Egypt (Exodus 2:11–15). The author of Hebrews makes the actions of Moses appear more deliberate, and he sees an act of faith in them. It was by faith, he tells us, Moses refused to be known as the son of the Pharaoh's daughter, rejecting the sinful luxuries of the court and choosing instead to share in the sufferings of his own people. He considered these sufferings by the people of Israel (God's Anointed) as more valuable than all the treasures of Egypt.

The author rapidly covers the Exodus event, telling us Moses, by his faith, had no fear of the Pharaoh but instead held firm like someone in direct contact with the invisible God. By faith, Moses celebrated the Passover, sprinkling the blood of the lamb so the angel of death would not kill the firstborn of the Israelites. The faith of the Israelites allowed them to cross the Red Sea, while the Egyptian soldiers who tried to cross the sea drowned. By faith, the Israelites entered the land of Canaan, and the walls of Jericho, after being encircled for seven days, collapsed (Joshua 6:1–27). The author commends Rahab, the prostitute, for her faith in harboring the spies from the Israelite camp (Joshua 2:1–23). Because of her faith, Rahab escaped the fate of those who lacked faith.

The author of Hebrews admits he can go on and on, recounting the actions of Israel's heroes which they performed with faith. He names judges, kings, and prophets, people such as Gideon, Barak, Samson, Jephthah, David, and Samuel. These judges, kings, and prophets were men who conquered kingdoms, did what was just, and obtained promises—all by faith. Alluding to Daniel, he states these heroes "closed the mouths of lions, put out raging fires, escaped the devouring sword" (11:33–34). Despite their weakness, these heroes were made more powerful by faith, becoming "strong in battle" and putting foreign armies to flight.

The author draws more examples from the Book of Maccabees and from the prophets. He lists the suffering of holy people for the sake of faith. Women received their dead back through resurrection. Because of their faith in a resurrection to a better life, some accepted torture and refused to accept release from their suffering. They were mocked, whipped, captured, stoned, stabbed, and tortured (11:36–37). They lived in deserts and caves. After listing all of these sufferings and the great rewards in store for those who lived by faith, the author concludes this passage in a surprising manner. He tells us, despite all of their suffering with faith, these heroes did not receive what was promised. God provided something better. Apart from us, they would not reach perfection. The author does not intend to say these heroes will not share the reward of their faith; rather, he is declaring that the plan of God reaches its perfection and proper fulfillment in Christ.

Lectio Divina

Spend 8 to 10 minutes in silent contemplation on the following passage:

The author of Hebrews defines faith as "the realization of what is hoped for and evidence of things not seen" (11:1). Although believers in God do not see God, they believe in God because of the evidence found in creation. Faith drove the heroes of the Old and New Testaments to be willing to sacrifice their lives or material well-being for the Lord.

In the Gospel of John, we read that Jesus appeared to his disciples on the night of his resurrection, but Thomas was not with them. When Thomas heard Jesus had appeared to the disciples, he declared he would not believe it unless he put his finger into Jesus' nail marks and his hand into his side. Jesus appeared to the disciples on the following Sunday and invited Thomas to touch his wounds and believe. When Thomas proclaims his faith, Jesus says, "Blessed are those who have not seen and have believed" (John 20:29). Throughout the ages, Christians have proclaimed that Jesus Christ had indeed been raised from the dead, and a countless number of Christians died for this belief.

Jesus' definition of faith would be God's blessing on those who have not seen the risen Christ but have believed.

✠ *What can I learn from this passage?*

Day 4: The Need for Obedience (12)

After offering witnesses by faith from the Old Testament, the author speaks to his listeners with the common New Testament image of a runner in a race. Just as runners carry as little weight as possible when running the race, so they should run the race steadfastly or, in other words, hold fast to the hope that comes from faith. They should not carry anything that hinders them from running the race well. Just as the runner keeps looking toward the finish line, so the author exhorts his listeners to keep their eyes set on Jesus. Since Jesus suffered and gave his blood to encourage his followers to live by faith, he is "the leader and perfecter of faith" (12:2).

The author teaches that Jesus refused to look on the cross as shameful, but endured it for the sake of the joy that lay in store for him. Jesus, whom they are to follow, has taken his rightful place at the right hand of the throne of God. By keeping Jesus as their focus, Christians can courageously withstand the opposition of sinners just as Jesus did. Although they have not yet shed their blood for their faith in Jesus, they should be ready to endure all for him.

The author then quotes from the Book of Proverbs (3:11–12), which states discipline from the Lord is a sign of God's love rather than an occasion for discouragement. He urges his listeners to be willing to endure their trials, knowing the Lord uses the trials for the sake of discipline. In this way, the Lord is treating them as God's children. The passage from Proverbs emphasizes that discipline enables a father to build his son's character. If a father does not discipline his son, then the son is not a real son.

Just as we are willing to accept discipline from our earthly fathers, so we should all the more be willing to accept discipline from our heavenly Father. Our earthly fathers disciplined us for our short, earthly life, while our heavenly Father disciplines us for our eternal good in order that we may share in his holiness. Discipline brings pain, not joy, but it later brings us peace and goodness. Keeping to his image of the runner, the author exhorts his listeners to strengthen themselves and to prepare a straight path. In this way their weakness, which he compares to lameness, will not become worse, but will instead be healed.

The author reminds his listeners they must act to achieve the Lord's gifts, teaching that these gifts do not become part of their lives simply because they wish for it. Instead they must strive for peace and holiness, working in such a way that no one loses the grace given by God. They must be careful no root of bitterness arises in their midst and defiles them. This is a reference to the Book of Deuteronomy, which speaks of those who contaminate the community in turning to false idols and drawing others with them (Deuteronomy 29:18).

A familiar story from the Old Testament is about Esau and Jacob, two brothers who serve as examples that God does not have to follow the human way of acting, but instead can choose the way of grace or blessings (Genesis 25). Esau, the elder son of Isaac, trades his right to the inheritance of the promise of God for a meal. When Isaac finally blesses Jacob, Esau tries to gain back his inheritance by begging his father for a blessing. Isaac can only give to Esau whatever blessing he has left, which does not include the inheritance of the promise made to Abraham and Isaac. The Israelites eventually see in Esau an example of every type of sin, including fornication, idolatry, and other images of a sinful life. Despite his pleading with tears, Esau is rejected, having lost any chance to repent.

The author contrasts the appalling events surrounding the old law with the encouraging gifts that come to us from God through Christ. In the Old Testament, Mount Sinai was the awesome place where God visited Moses. The people were afraid to touch the mountain, and certain laws even prohibited animals from drawing near it, with stoning to death as the consequence. They spoke of the mountain in dreadful and frightening terms, calling it untouchable, "a blazing fire and gloomy darkness and storm and a trumpet blast," and other words of terror that brought destruction to those who heard them (12:18–19). The fear and trembling surrounding the giving of the old law was so great that even Moses experienced it.

The people addressed in Hebrews, however, do not have these fears that accompanied God's presence during the time of the Exodus. They can confidently approach the new mountain of the Lord—"Mount Zion and the city of the living God, the heavenly Jerusalem"—where "God the judge of all, and...Jesus, the mediator of a new covenant" dwell (12:22–24). Here the spilled blood of Christ pleads more insistently than Abel's, which called out to God from the earth after Cain killed him. The blood of Christ is the blood of purification rather than that of condemnation.

The author contrasts the people's response to the old law with the new. If the Israelites could not escape from God who spoke to them from the earth, the author questions, how much more shall his readers be punished if they do not listen to the One who speaks from heaven? In the past, God's voice made the earth shake, but now, in the New Jerusalem, the heavens as well as the earth will shake. That which can be shaken—namely, that which belongs to the created universe—will cease, while that which cannot be shaken—namely, the heavenly realm—will remain.

As Christians, we have received the gift of an unshakable, and therefore eternal, kingdom. This should encourage us to remain faithful to the grace we have received and to use it to worship God in an acceptable manner, with reverence and awe.

Lectio Divina

Spend 8 to 10 minutes in silent contemplation of the following passage:

Christians must always be conscious of the presence of Christ in their lives, just as runners keep their eyes on the goal. Christ is our goal, the one who lives in our heart and mind each day of our life and the one toward whom we run with the hope of eternal life. When we encounter struggles and temptations in our life that attempt to distract us from the goal, we must strive not to allow them to divert us from the path to Christ. As Christians, we believe Christ is always ready to help us. He is the companion in the race and the goal toward which we run. We live in peace and love, knowing Christ, who died for us, is guiding us to our final end.

✠ *What can I learn from this passage?*

Day 5: Exhortations, Blessings, Greetings (13)

Some commentators consider Chapter Twelve to be the end of the Letter to the Hebrews, believing this last chapter is an appendix added by a later editor. Although Chapter Twelve seems to conclude what the author has to say, most commentators still believe this chapter (13) was written by the original author as an ending to the letter.

The author begins this chapter by instructing his readers how they should live as Christians. He exhorts them to love one another and to treat one another with hospitality, always aware they could be entertaining angels instead of human beings. This is a reference to the Book of Genesis, which speaks of Abraham and Lot showing hospitality to angels who each thought were human beings (Genesis 18:1–8; 19:1–3).

The author urges his readers to care for those in prison as though they themselves were in prison, and to have concern for those who are being tortured as though they themselves were being tortured. He states they are also in the body, a possible reference to the Body of Christ, the Church. They should hold marriage in high esteem and not defile the marriage bed; otherwise they will face God's judgment as fornicators and adulterers. They should learn to accept what they have, not greedily seeking more, but be content with the idea that God will not desert them (Deuteronomy 31:6). The author quotes from Psalm 118:6, stating the Lord is our helper and we have no reason to fear what anyone can do to us.

The author urges his readers to remember their leaders who preached God's Word and gave them an example of faith to follow. Although these leaders may die, the central theme of their preaching revolves around Jesus, who will always remain the same yesterday, today, and forever.

The author warns his readers against chasing after strange teachings and urges them to rely on the grace of God for their inner strength rather than on food, a reference to the Jewish laws concerning abstinence from certain foods. The author states that these rules have failed to help those who followed them.

Christians have their own altar, namely Christ. Those who serve the tabernacle according to the old law have no right to partake of the sacrifice of this altar. The author of Hebrews is teaching that the New Covenant broke with the Old, and the Old has no part in the New. In the old law, animals sacrificed as sin offerings were not eaten in the sacrificial meal, but were burnt outside the city (Leviticus 16:27). In the same way, the sin offering of the New Covenant, Christ, was sacrificed outside the city of Jerusalem. Christians are invited to leave the tabernacle, the Old Covenant, and symbolically to go outside the city with Christ to share in his humiliation. Going outside the city implies that the New Covenant does not provide us with a city here on earth, but prepares us for the life to come.

Through Christ, the author calls Christians to offer a sacrifice of praise to God, one that is offered by our words each time we acknowledge God's name, rather than the animal sacrifices of the old law. We should also perform good works and share what we have, since these sacrifices are pleasing to God.

The author, most likely a leader of the people himself, urges his listeners to obey their leaders. He points out leaders must give an account of the way they looked after those entrusted to their care. Cooperation is a source of joy for the community's leaders and saves everyone grief.

The author requests the prayers of his readers and states he lives with a clear conscience. This request may be an indication he is in prison, yet is not ashamed of his humiliation. His intent is to behave honorably in all situations. He finds hope in their prayers, viewing the prayers as a means of bringing him to them more quickly. Although most commentators do not believe Paul wrote this letter, the ending sounds as if Paul is truly the author of this letter.

The author prays that the God of peace will make those for whom this letter is intended respond to God's will in everything they do. He states that God "brought [Jesus] up from the dead," perhaps a reference to the resurrection or to Christ's call to heavenly glory (13:20). In either case, the author proclaims Christ, through the blood of the eternal covenant, is "the great shepherd of the sheep," a reference from Isaiah 63:11, which speaks of Moses being raised up from the Red Sea as the shepherd of the sheep (the chosen leader of the Israelites). The author prays his listeners will please God through Jesus Christ, who is worthy of eternal glory.

He ends by asking his readers to accept his brief words of advice in a friendly manner, and he gives them news Timothy has been set free. Timothy is mentioned as Paul's beloved companion by the apostle himself, but the author makes no statement concerning his relationship with Timothy. The author's use of Timothy's name here could be another way of adding authenticity to his words. The author expresses his hope Timothy will join him when he visits them, and he offers greetings to all the leaders and the saints (all Christians). He sends greetings from those who come from Italy. This could mean the letter comes from Italy, possibly Rome, or that the author has companions with him who are from Italy. Instead of wishing them the grace of our Lord Jesus Christ, which is a common Pauline ending, the author ends with the simple prayer for grace.

Lectio Divina

Spend 8 to 10 minutes in silent contemplation of the following passage:

At the beginning of this last chapter, the author exhorts his readers to allow mutual love to continue, and he presents several ways his readers may do this. The message of sharing mutual love echoes the words of Jesus, who told his disciples, "'You shall love the Lord your God with all your heart, with all your soul, with all your mind, and with all your strength.' The second is like this: 'You shall love your neighbor as yourself'" (Mark 12:30–31). After informing the reader throughout his letter about Jesus Christ, our eternal high priest who gave himself as the everlasting sacrifice for us, it is fitting the author's final message echoes the central message of love taught by Jesus.

✠ *What can I learn from this passage?*

Review Questions

1. How do the regulations for worship in the first covenant compare with those of the New Covenant?

2. Why is Christ considered the mediator of the New Covenant?

3. What, according to the author of Hebrews, makes the one sacrifice of the New Covenant sufficient?

4. Why does the author recall the past for the reader?

5. What is the faith of the ancients and how does it compare with the faith of the New Covenant people?

6. Why does God allow us to be disciplined through suffering?

7. What are some ways in which Christians can show mutual love for one another?

About the Author

William A. Anderson, DMin, PhD, is a presbyter of the Diocese of Wheeling-Charleston, West Virginia. A director of retreats and parish missions, professor, catechist, spiritual director, and a former pastor, he has written extensively on pastoral, spiritual, and religious subjects. Father Anderson earned his doctor of ministry degree from St. Mary's Seminary & University in Baltimore, and his doctorate in sacred theology from Duquesne University in Pittsburgh.

THE *LIGUORI CATHOLIC BIBLE STUDY* SERIES INCLUDES THE FOLLOWING TITLES—AND MORE!

Introduction to the Bible:
Overview, Historical Context, and Cultural Perspectives
ISBN 978-0-7648-2119-6 • 112 pages

The Gospel of Matthew: Proclaiming the Ministry of Jesus
ISBN 978-0-7648-2120-2 • 160 pages

The Gospel of Luke: Salvation for All Humanity
ISBN 978-0-7648-2122-6 • 144 pages

The Gospel of John: The Word Became Flesh
ISBN 978-0-7648-2123-3 • 144 pages

The Acts of the Apostles: Good News for All People
ISBN 978-0-7648-2124-0 • 144 pages

Letters to the Corinthians: Gifts of the Holy Spirit
ISBN 978-0-7648-2126-4 • 144 pages

Paul's Early and Prison Letters: 1 and 2 Thessalonians,
Philippians, Colossians, Ephesians, Philemon
ISBN 978-0-7648-2127-1 • 144 pages

Letters to the Romans and Galatians:
Reconciling the Old and New Covenants
ISBN 978-0-7648-2125-7 • 144 pages

Historical Books I: Joshua, Judges, Ruth, 1 and 2 Samuel
ISBN 978-0-7648-2133-2 • 144 pages

Historical Books II:
1 and 2 Kings, 1 and 2 Chronicles, Ezra, Nehemiah
ISBN 978-0-764821349 • 144 pages

Also available in Spanish and eBook formats
For more information, visit Liguori.org or call 800-325-9521.

CPSIA information can be obtained
at www.ICGtesting.com
Printed in the USA
FFOW04n0216240214
3772FF

9 780764 821288